interludes

Anne Bjerge Hansen

Entr'acte

In the everyday run of events, en route to who knows where in particular, a random image will sometimes capture our attention, and hold us briefly under its spell. A glimpse of a human figure might do it, silhouetted in graceful mechanical motion behind panes of frosted glass. Or, a cameo from nature, perhaps — water lapping in the wake of a speedboat; a solitary flower buffeted in the wind. Or, among more familiar surroundings, a humdrum object or action, hitherto unnoticed, that only now impinges on consciousness. Fragments of reality that take on the quality of reverie. God is in the details, they say; and it is in the details that Anne Bjerge Hansen excels.

In her ongoing series of video interludes, this Danish-born, Glasgow-based artist offers a vivid visual index of these haunting and ephemeral moments. Deceptively simple but immaculately composed, Bjerge Hansen's subtly unfolding moving-image tableaux play with the conventions of the still life and the landscape, but, most of all, with the viewer's expectations, hatching droll and disarming micro-dramas from the brimming minutiae of life. Drawn to in-between spaces, to transitory phenomena, to the subtleties and nuances of things, Bjerge Hansen's interludes insinuate themselves gently but continue to reverberate in the mind. Supreme within the boundaries of her small-scale world, it is testimony to her skill as an artist that she makes it seem such an enchanting place to be.

The DVD edition of *Interludes* brings together a number of the pieces that Bjerge Hansen has accumulated over the course of the last few years, and combines them with new works completed during 2003. Released to accompany the Film and Video Umbrella touring exhibition of the same name, produced in collaboration with Angel Row Gallery, Nottingham, ArtSway and Focal Point Gallery, Southend-on-Sea, it showcases a number of newly-commissioned pieces shot in and around the host locations. We are grateful to the National Touring Programme of Arts Council England for their support of this project, and to the Scottish Arts Council for their important contribution to this accompanying publication.

Steven Bode

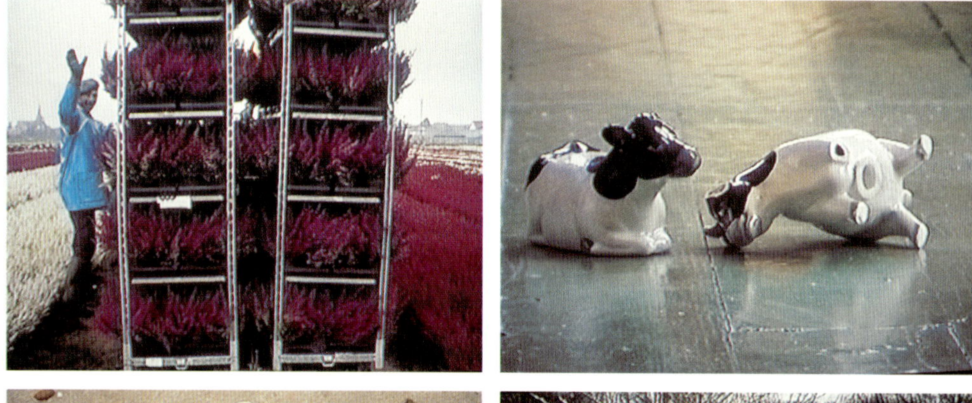

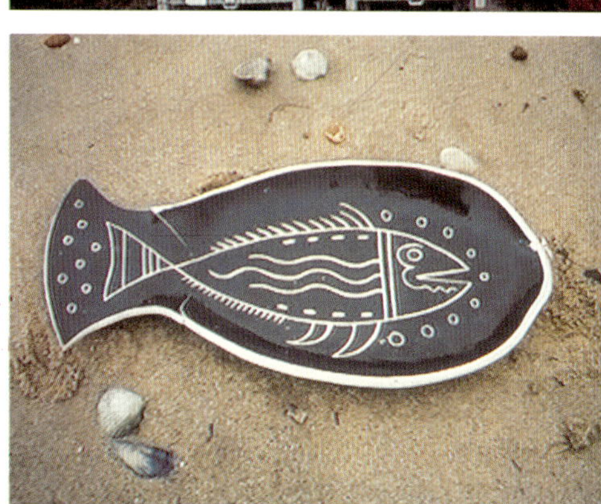

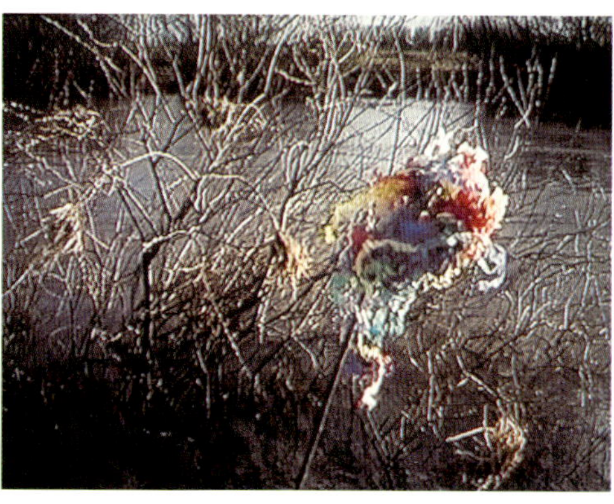

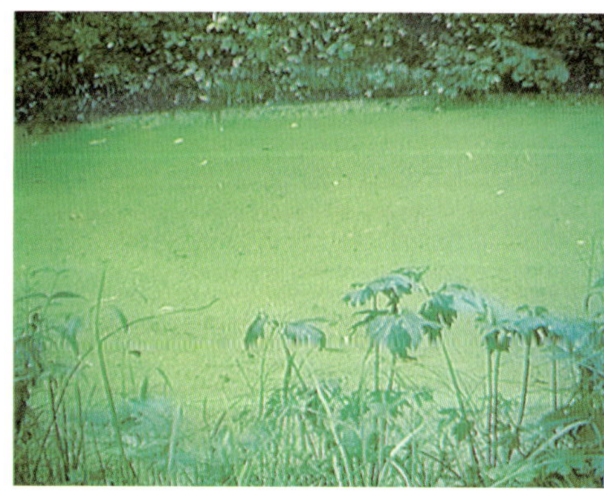

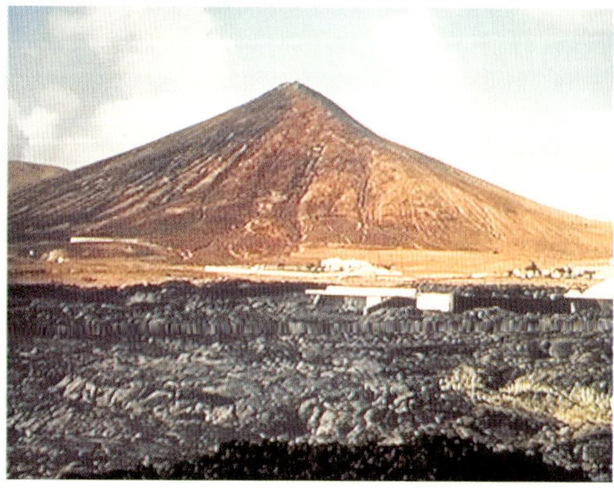

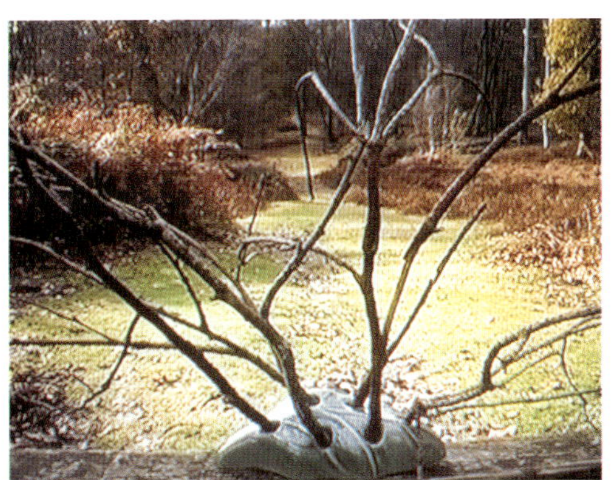
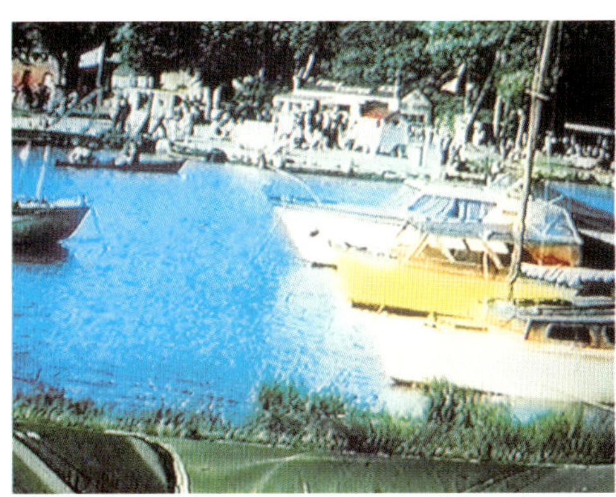
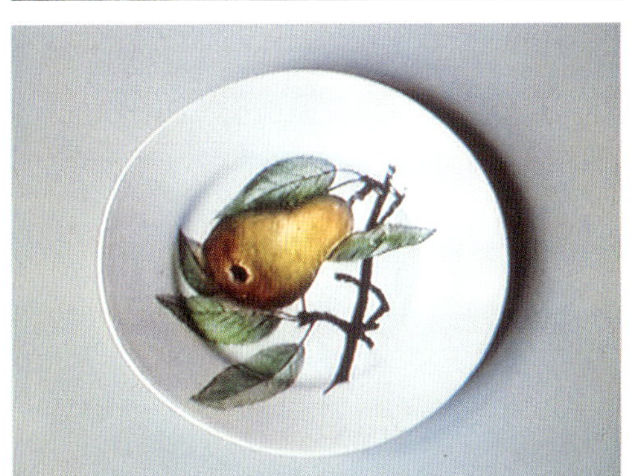
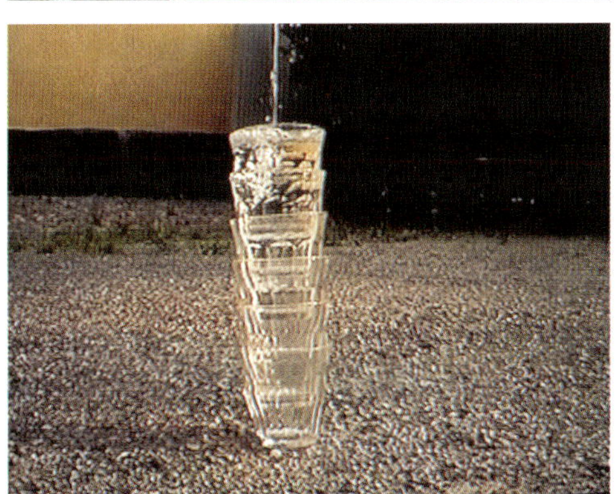
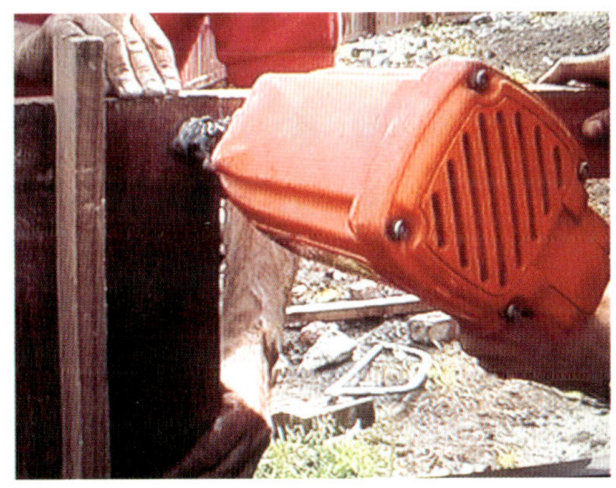
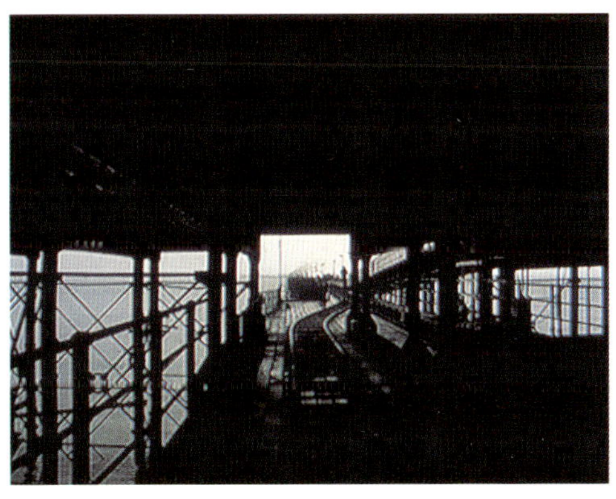

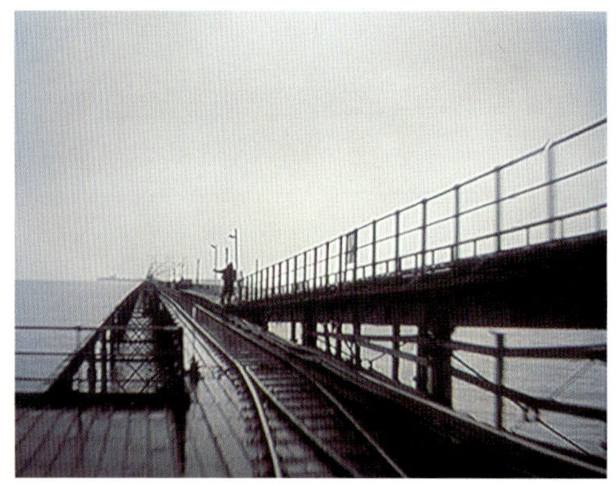
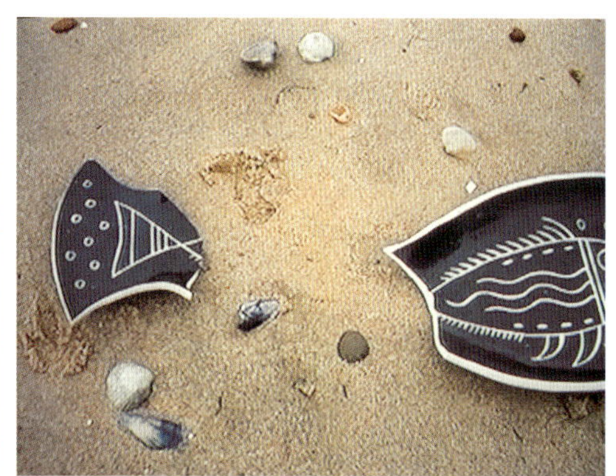
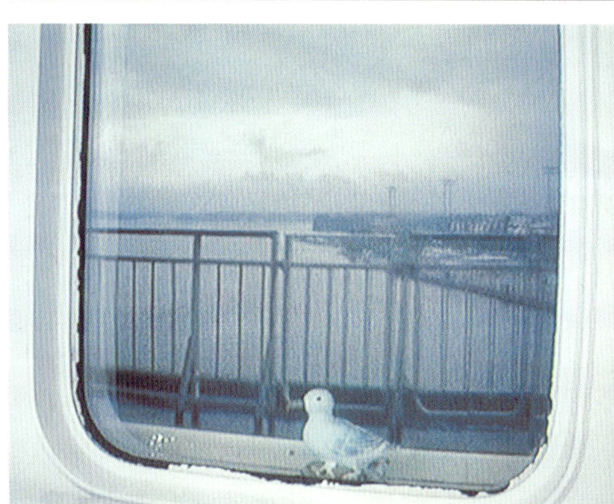
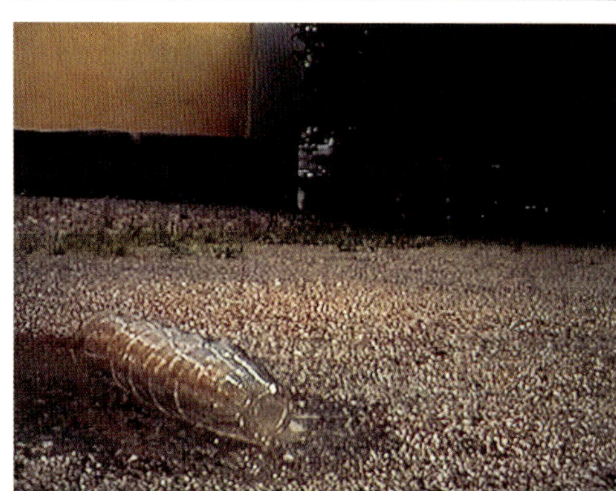
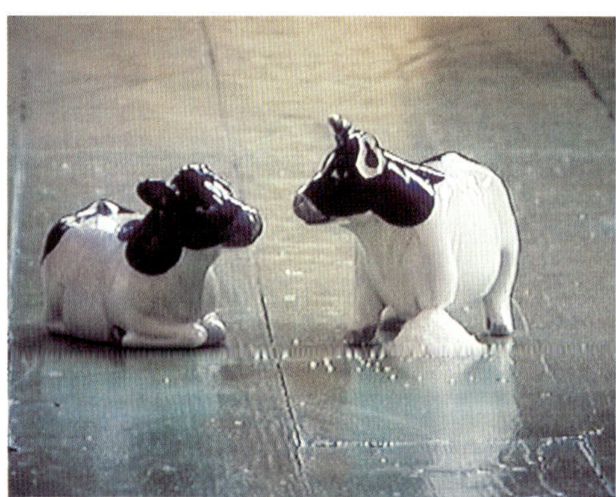
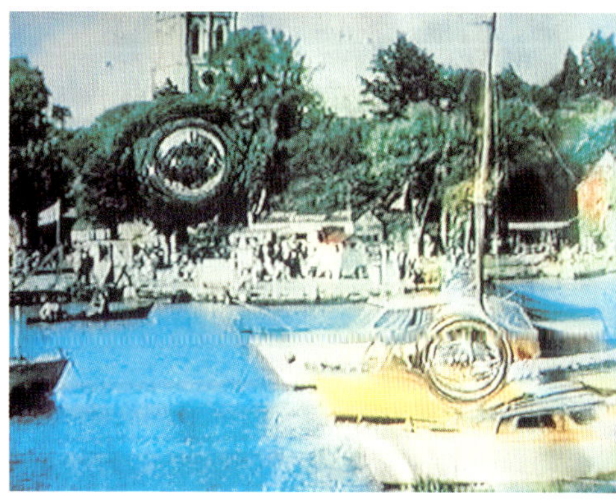

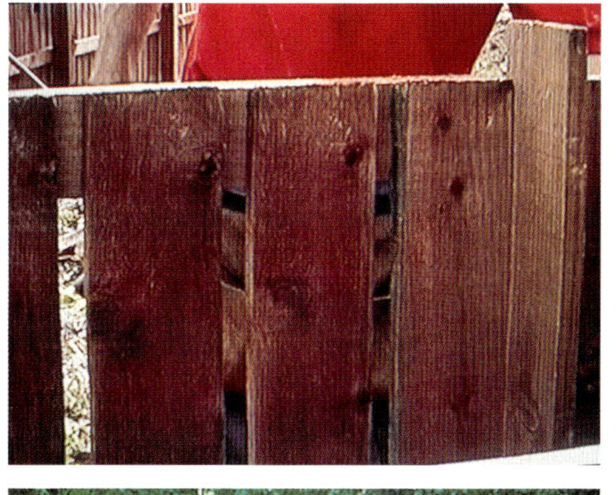

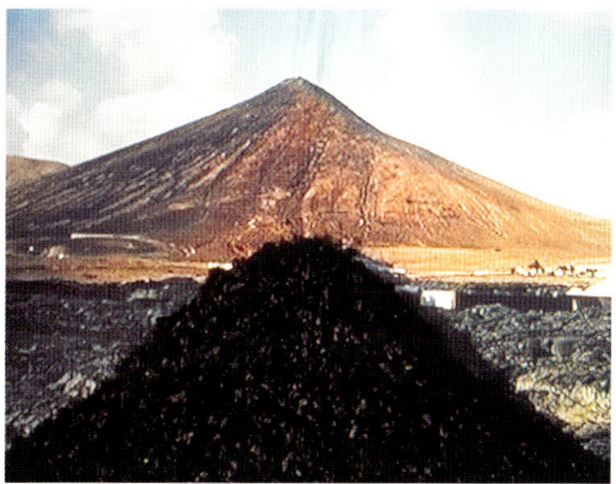

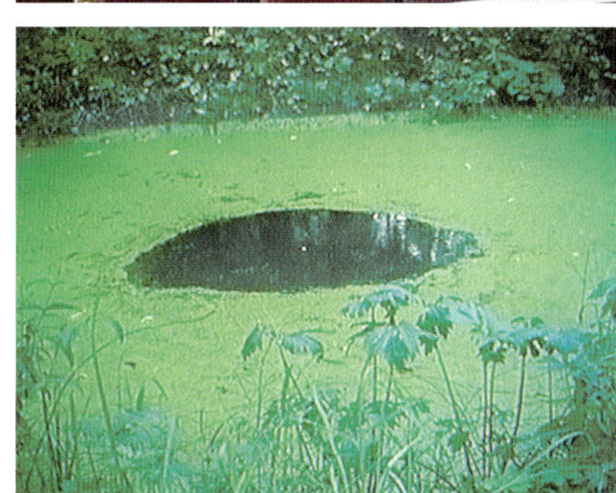

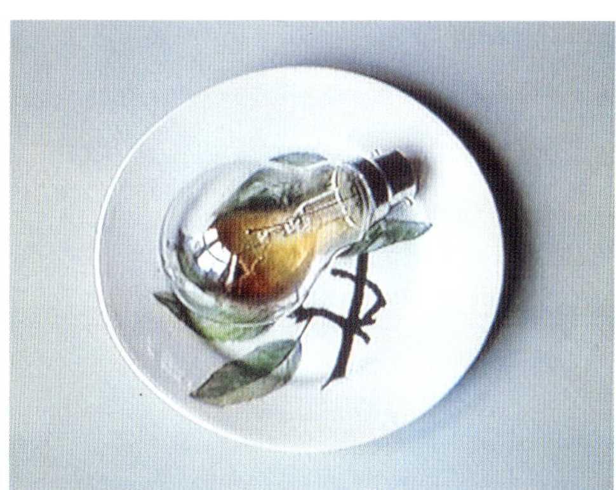

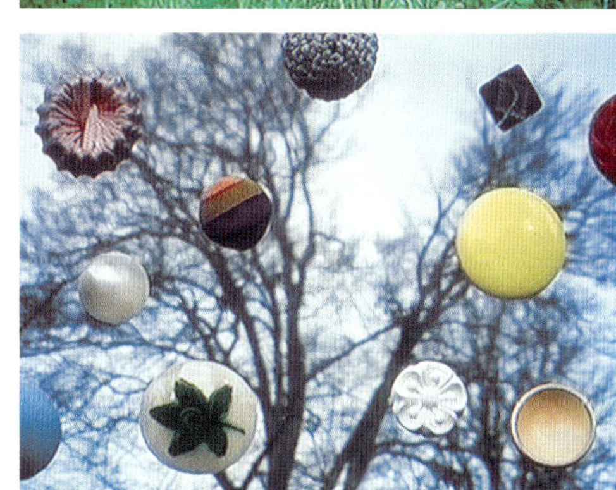

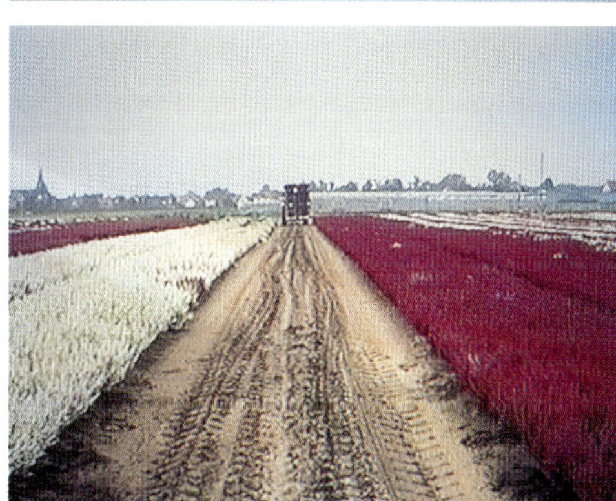

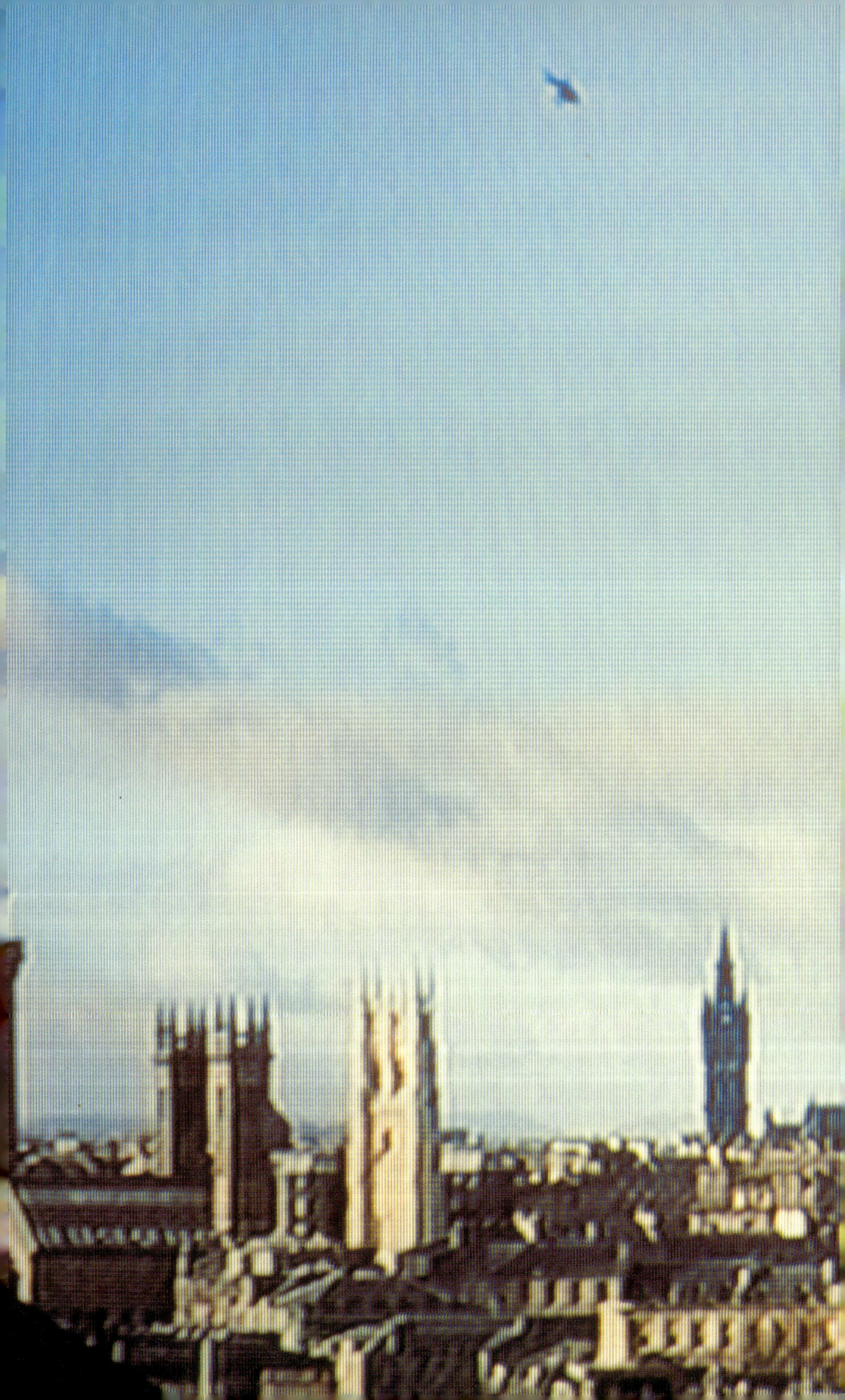

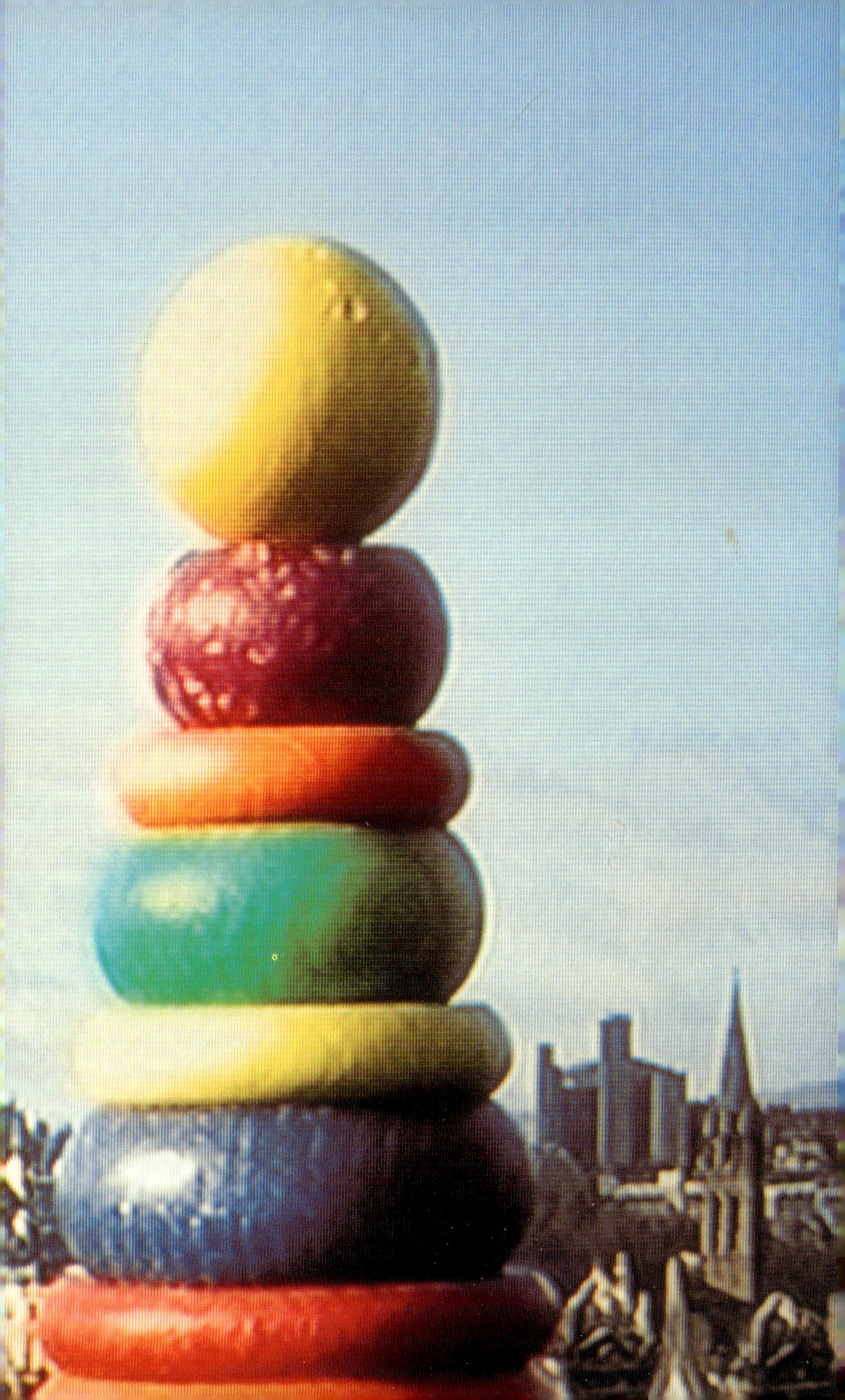

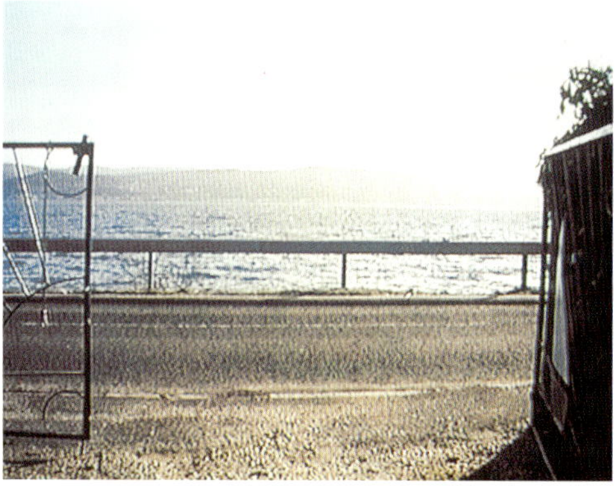

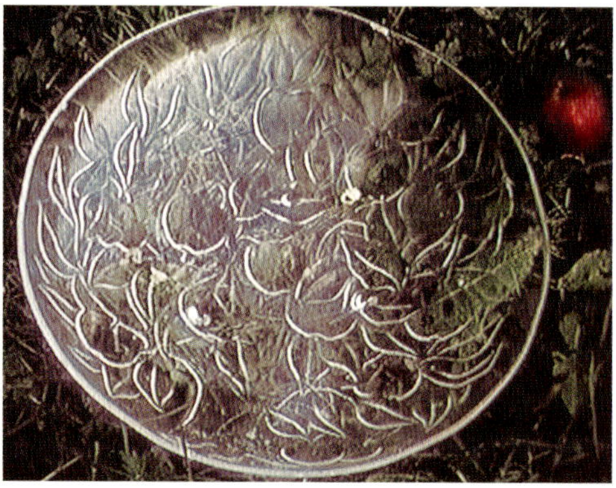

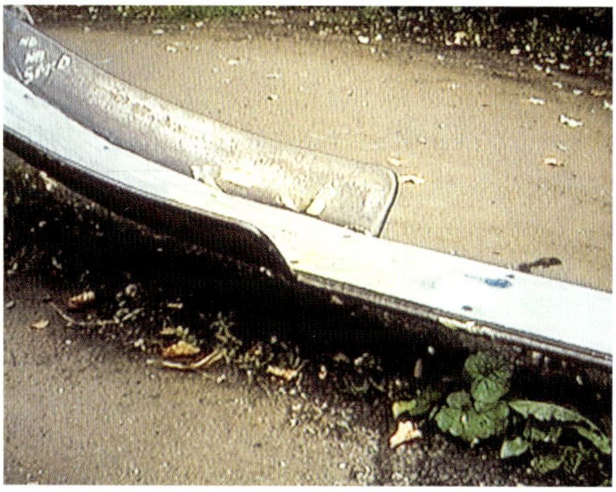

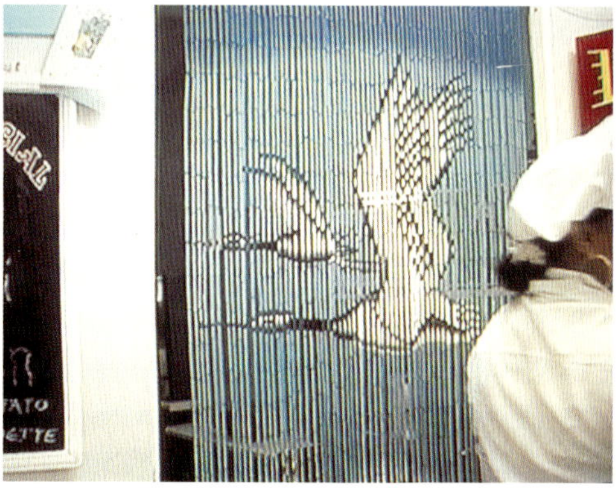

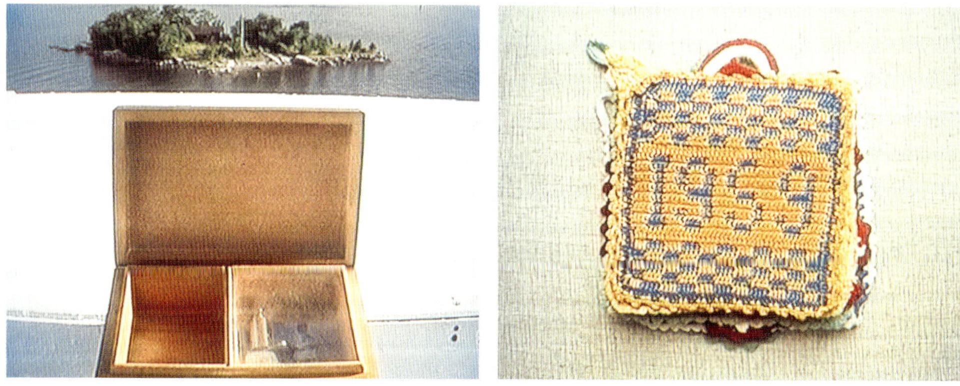

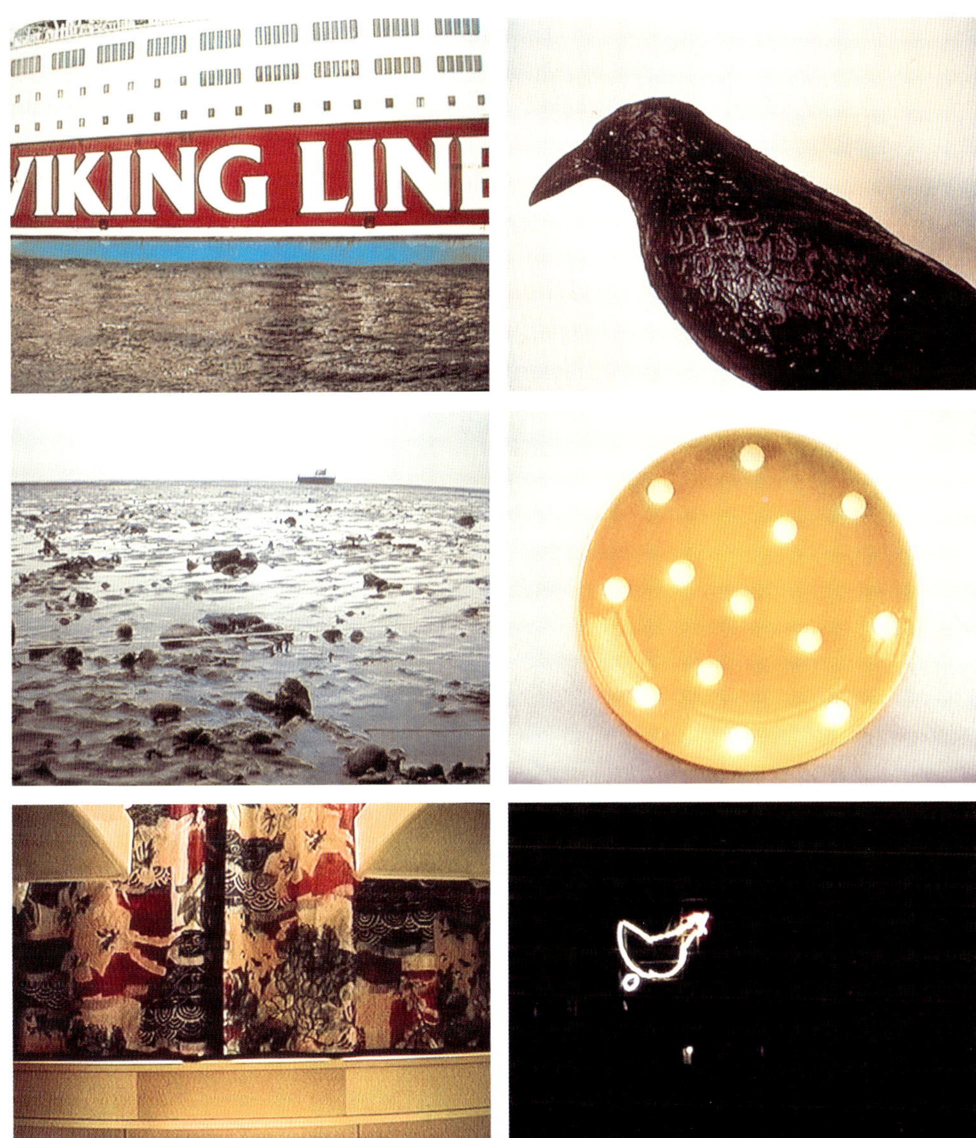
VIKING LINE

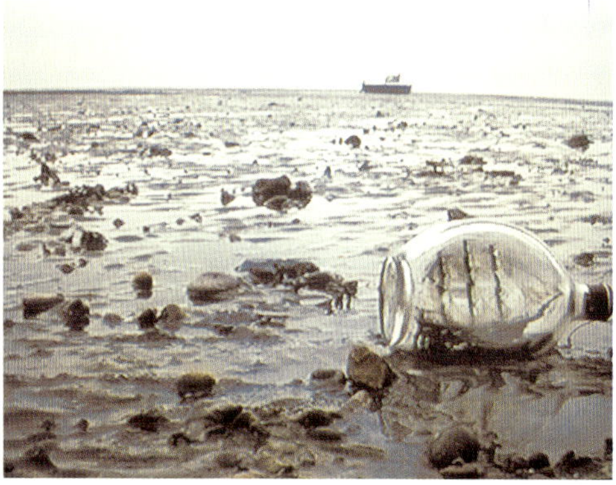

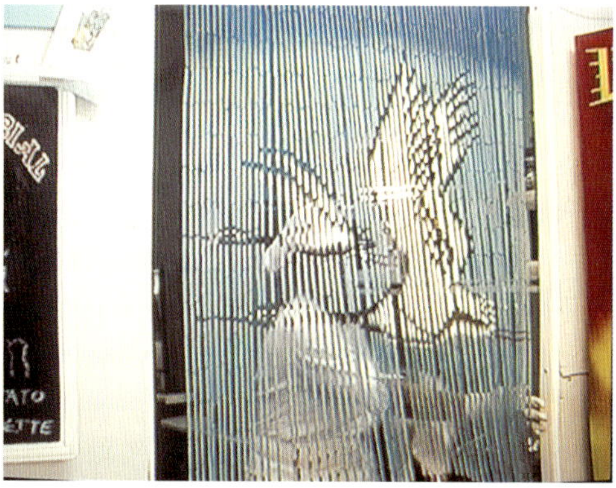

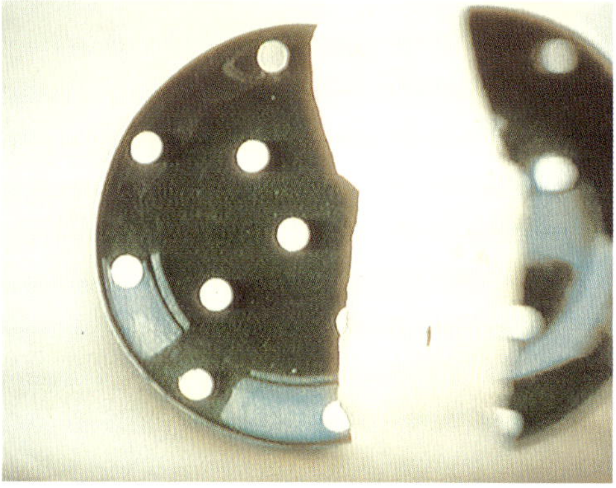

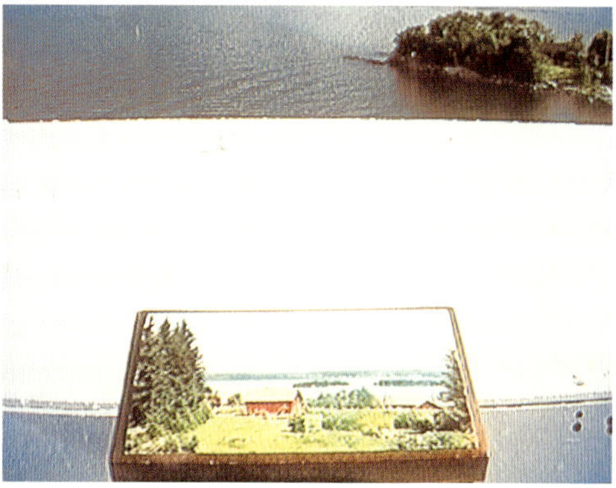

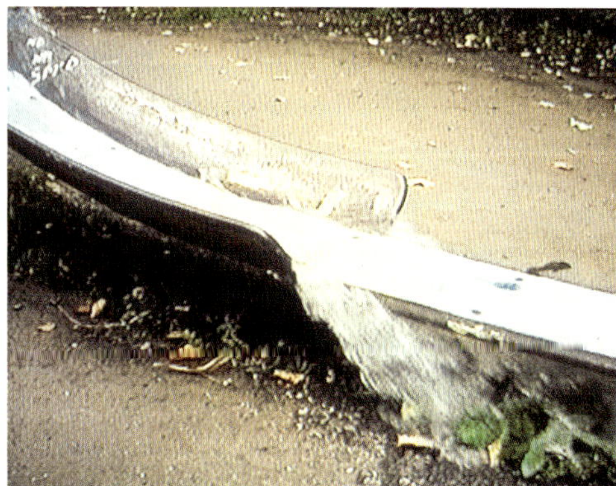

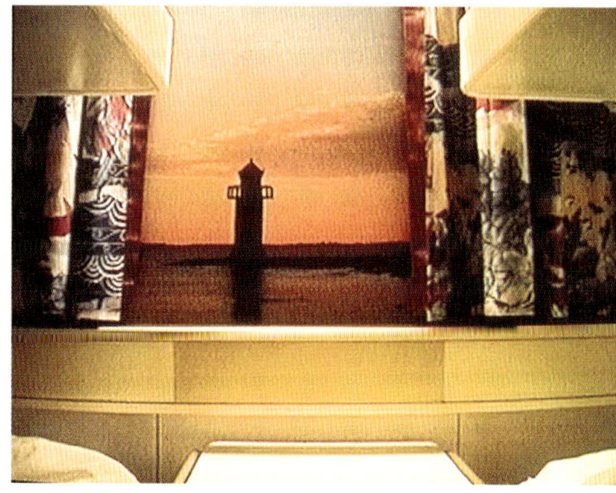

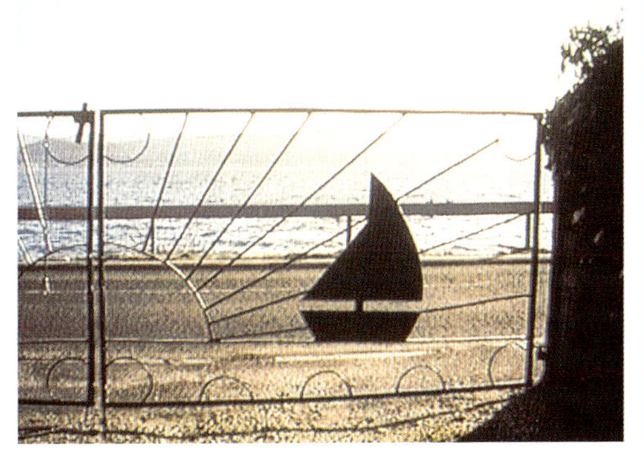

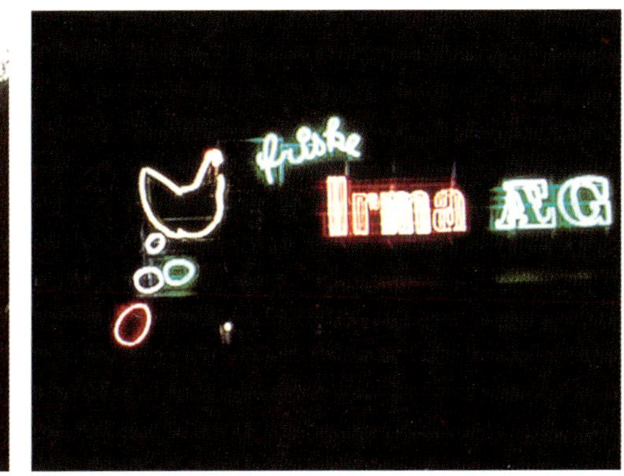
friske
Irma ÆG

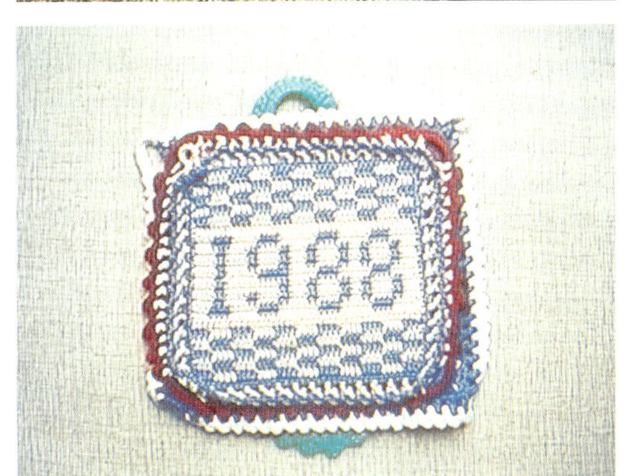
1988

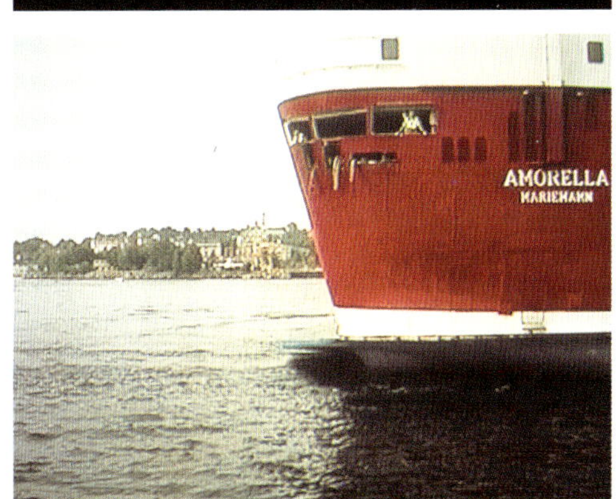
AMORELLA
MARIEHAMN

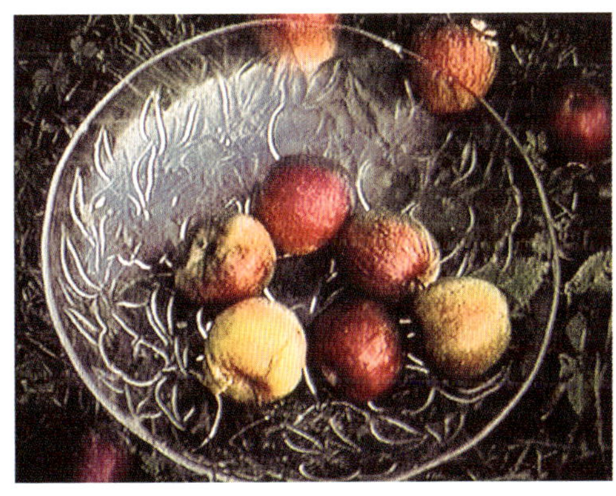

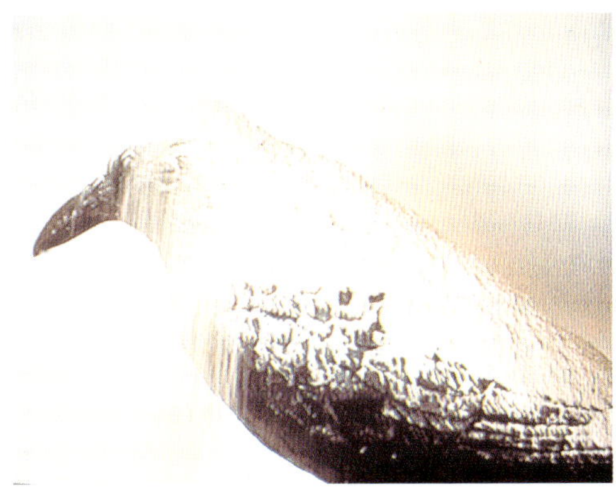

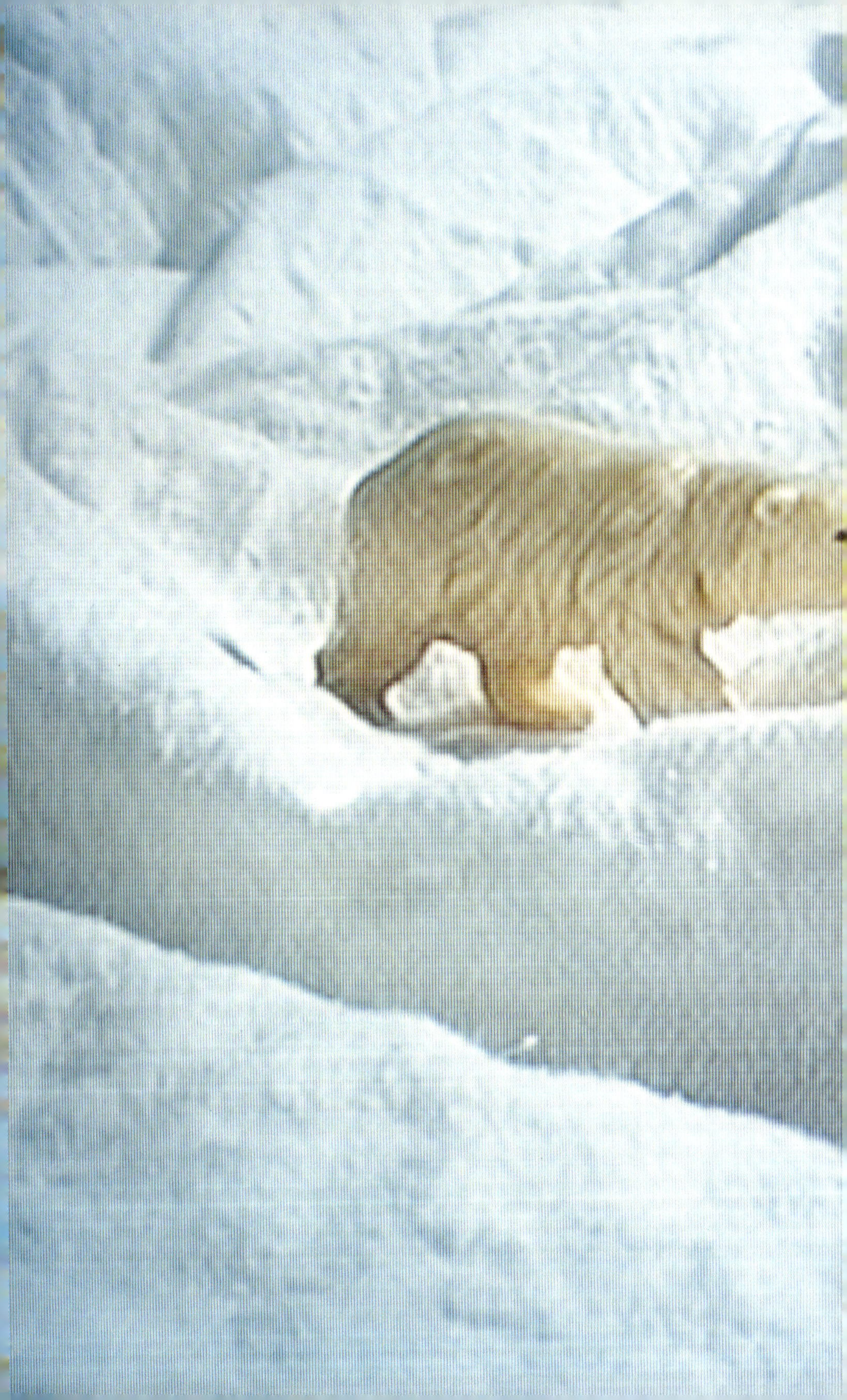

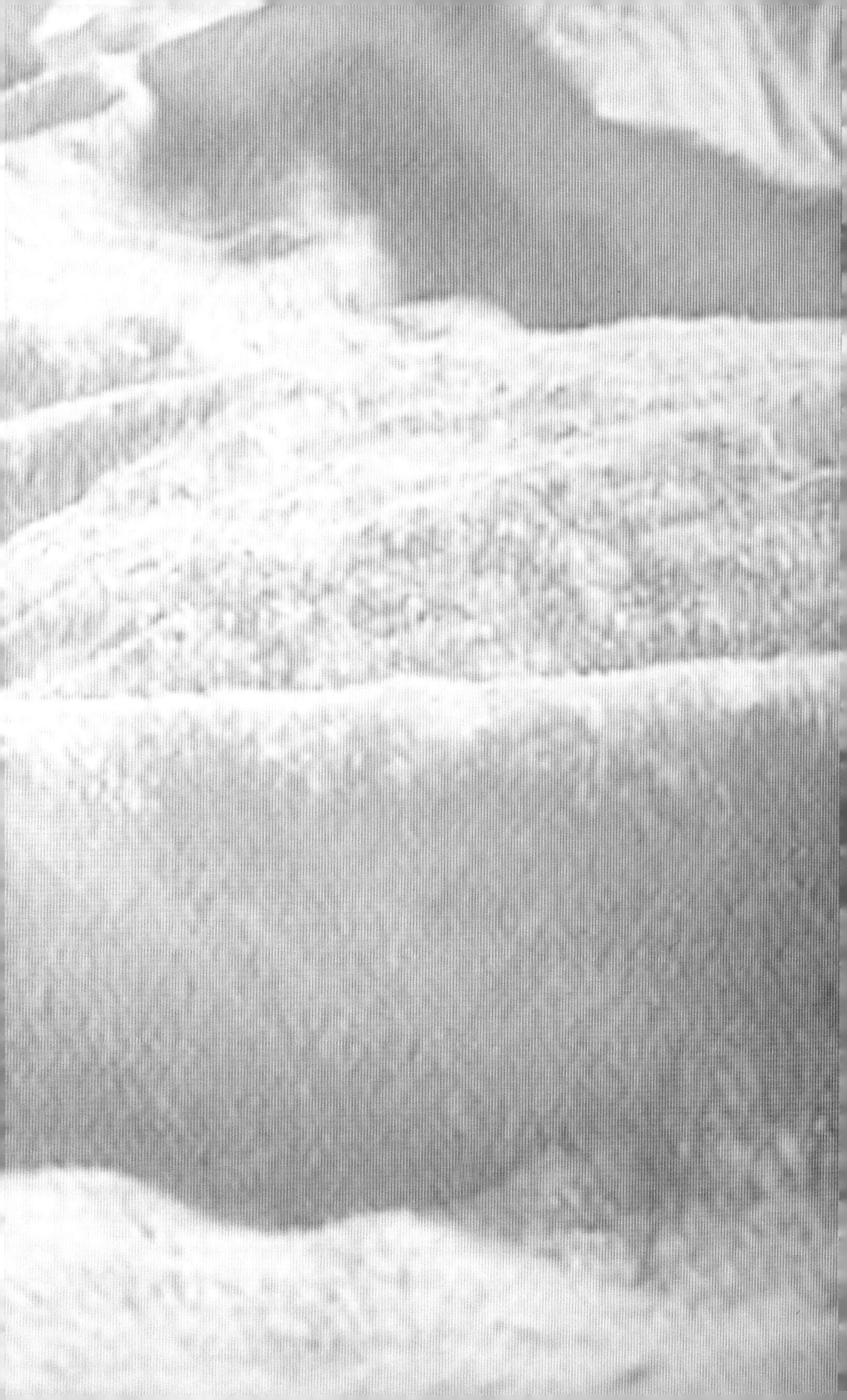

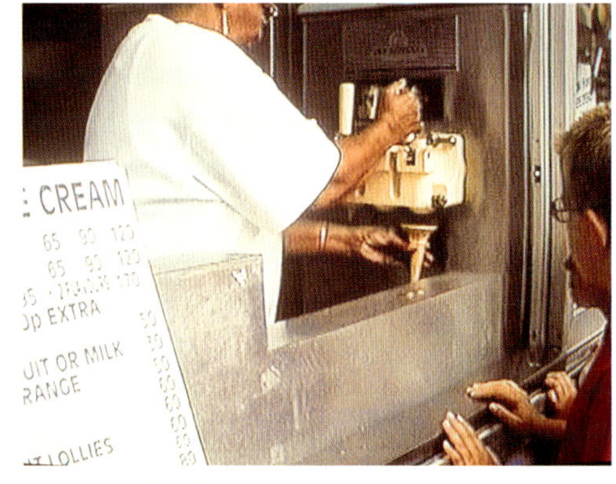
E CREAM
65 90 120
65 90 120
OP EXTRA
UIT OR MILK
RANGE

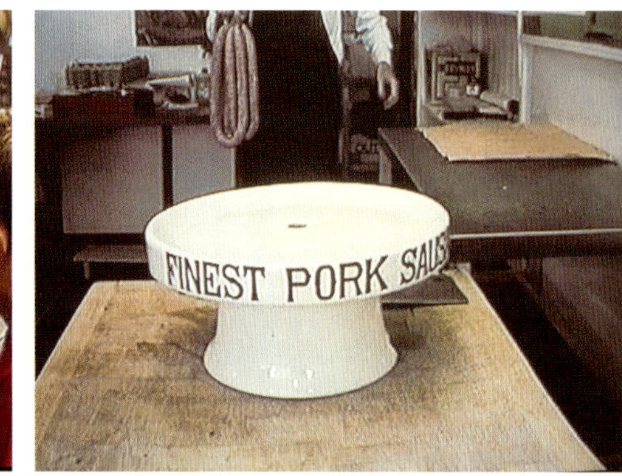
FINEST PORK SAU

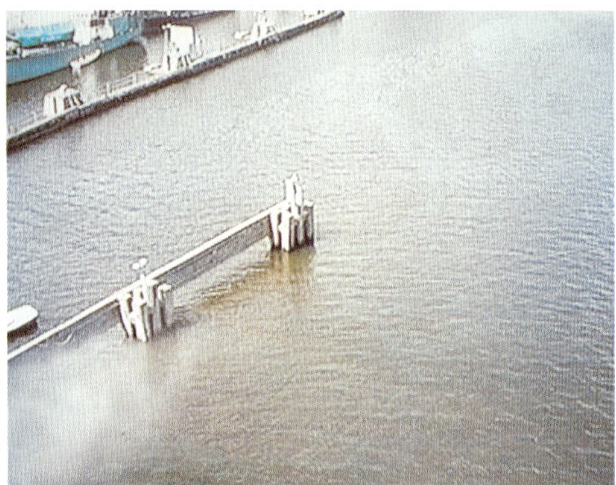

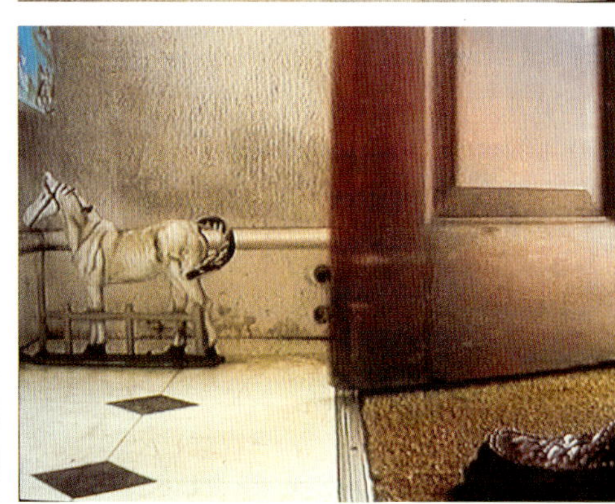

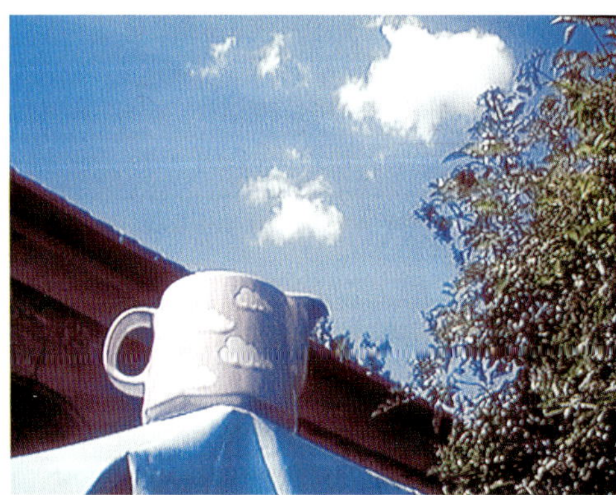

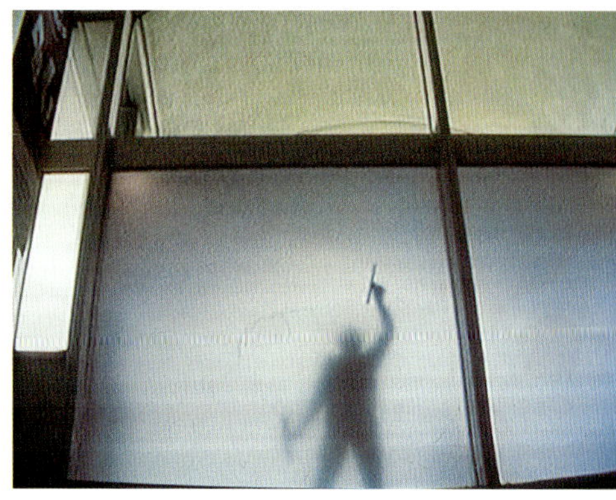

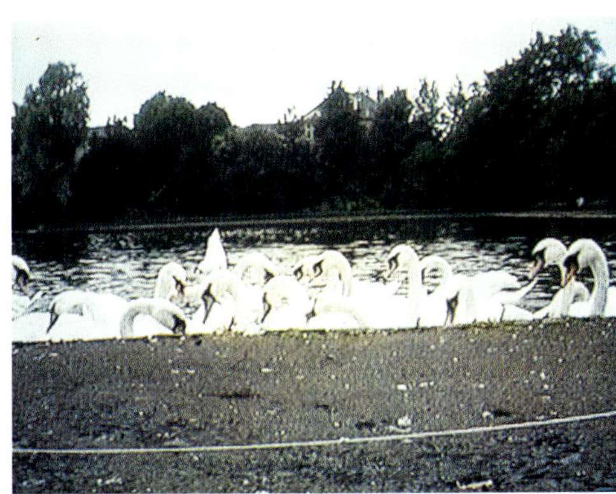

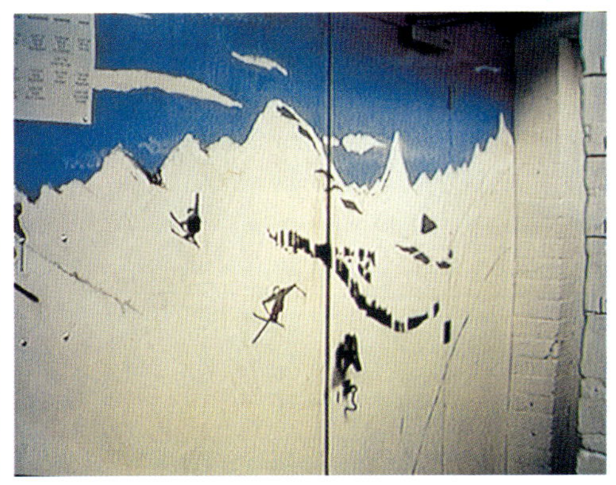

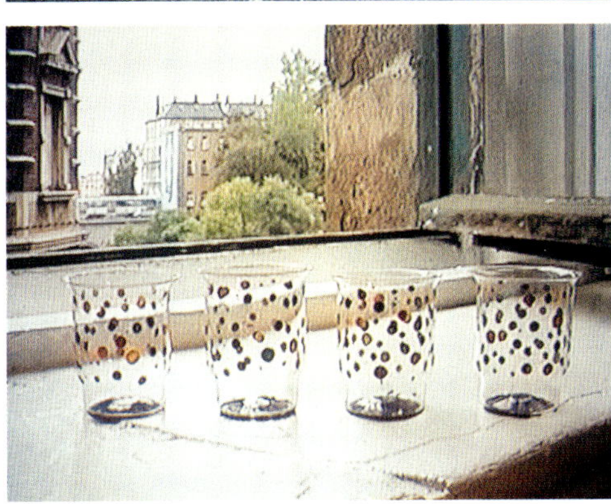

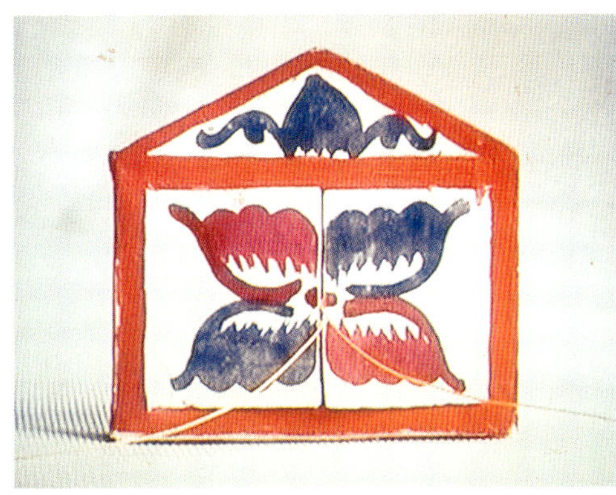

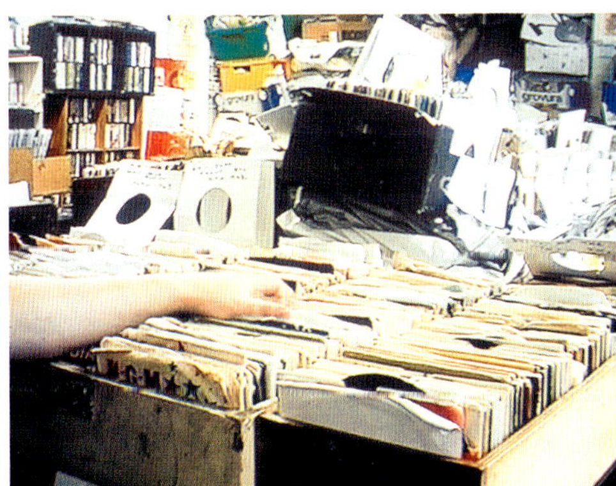

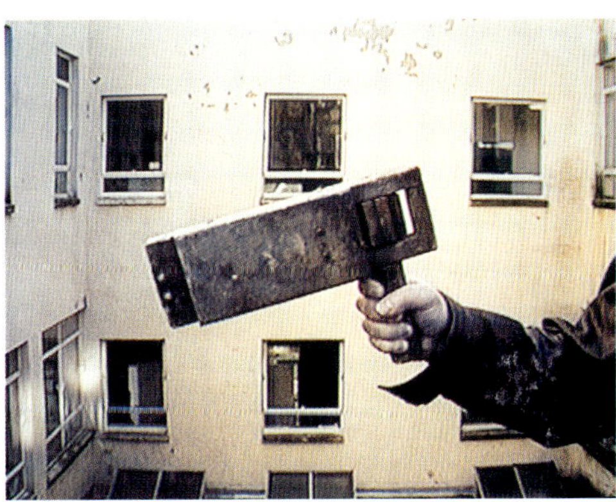

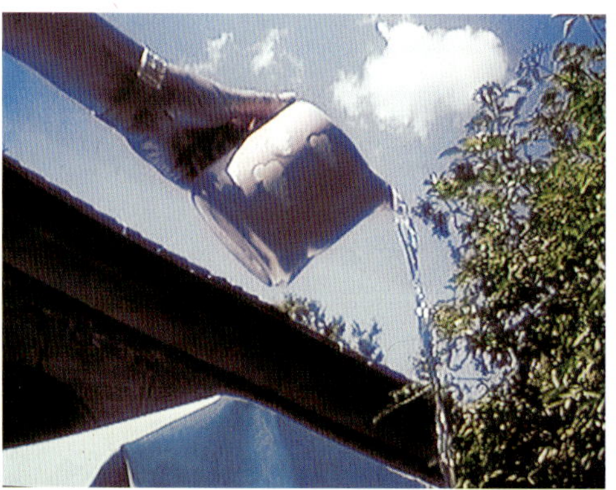

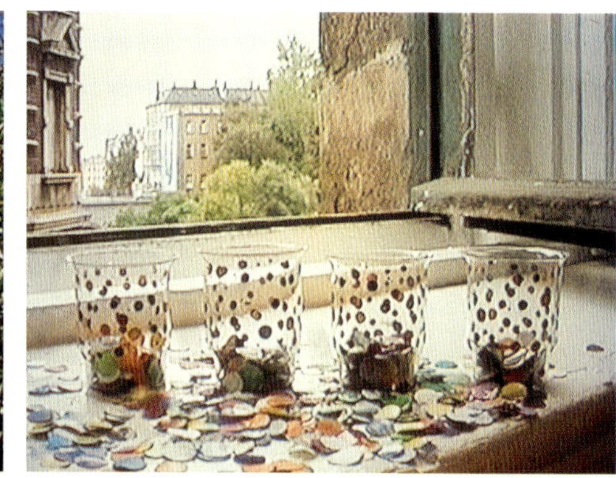

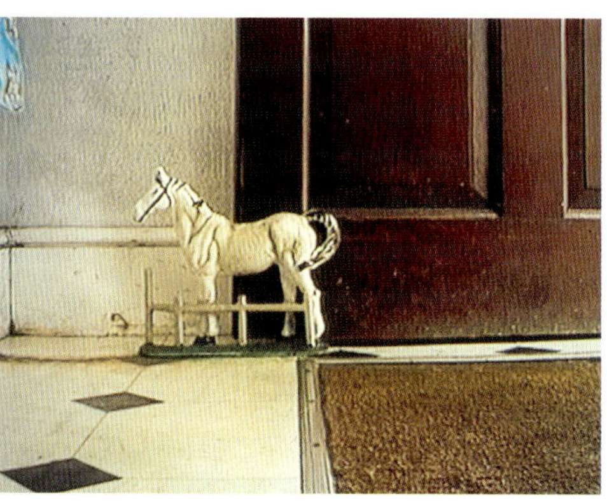

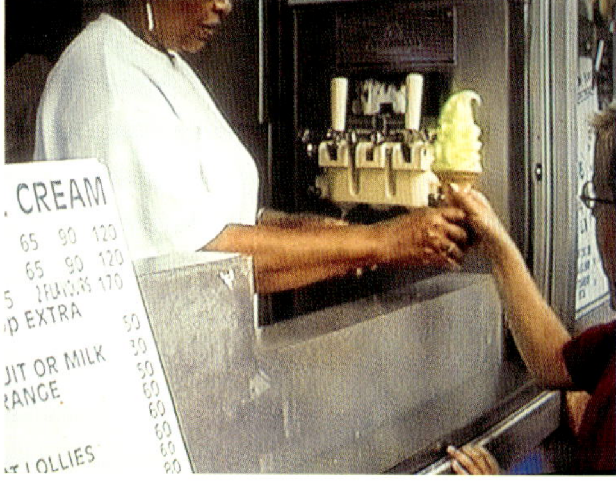
CREAM
65 90 120
65 90 120
170
EXTRA 50
30
OR MILK 50
60
60
60
60
LOLLIES 80

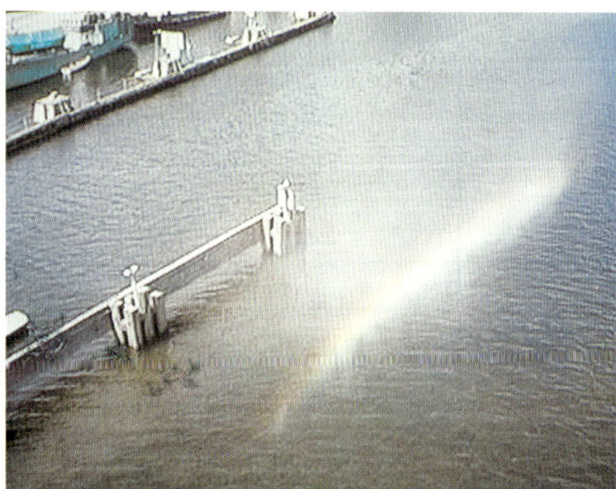

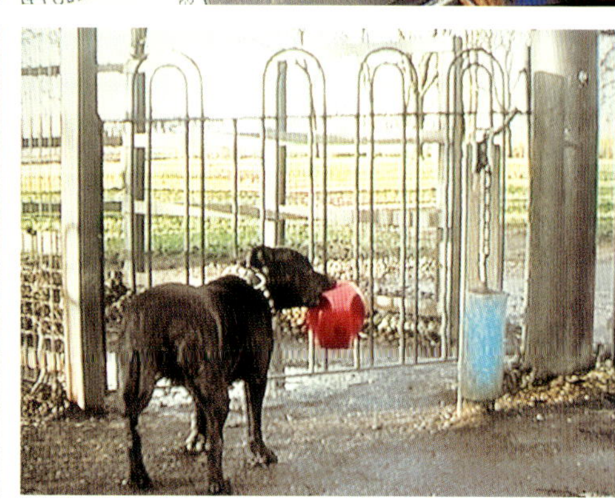

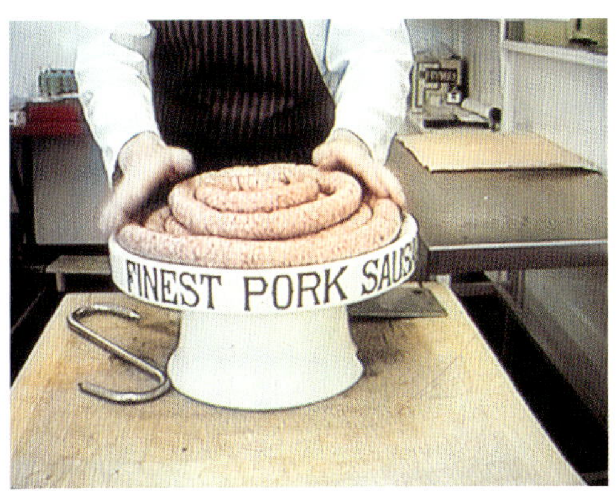
FINEST PORK

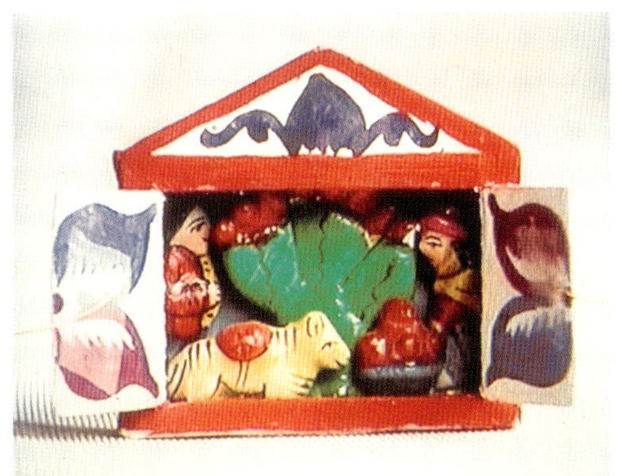

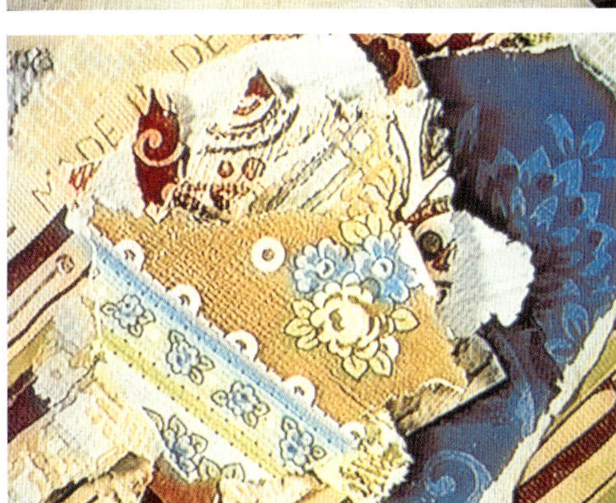

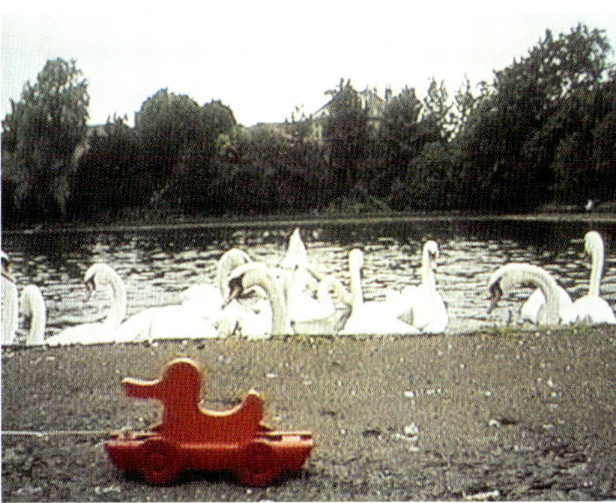

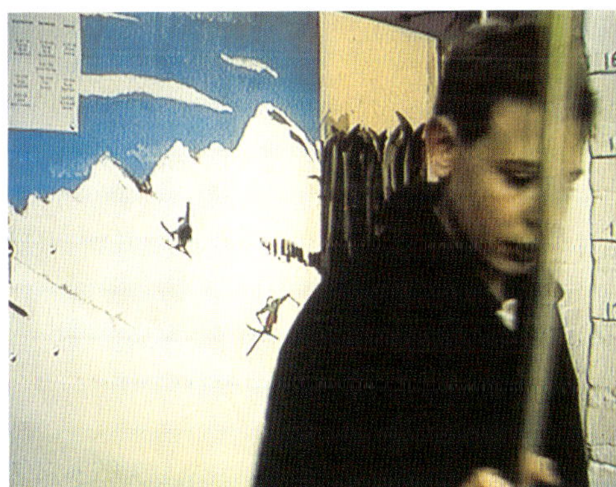

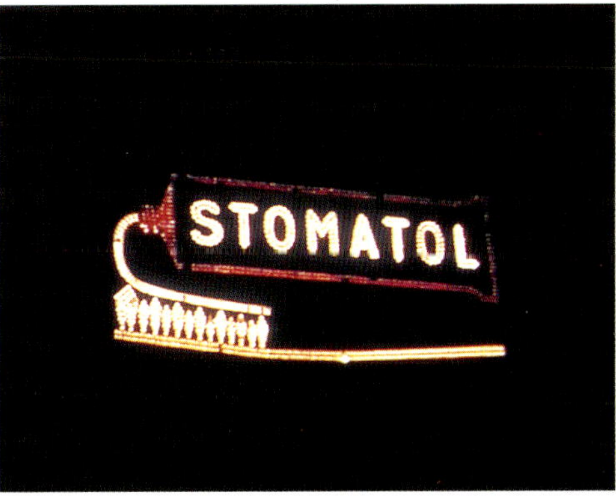
STOMATOL

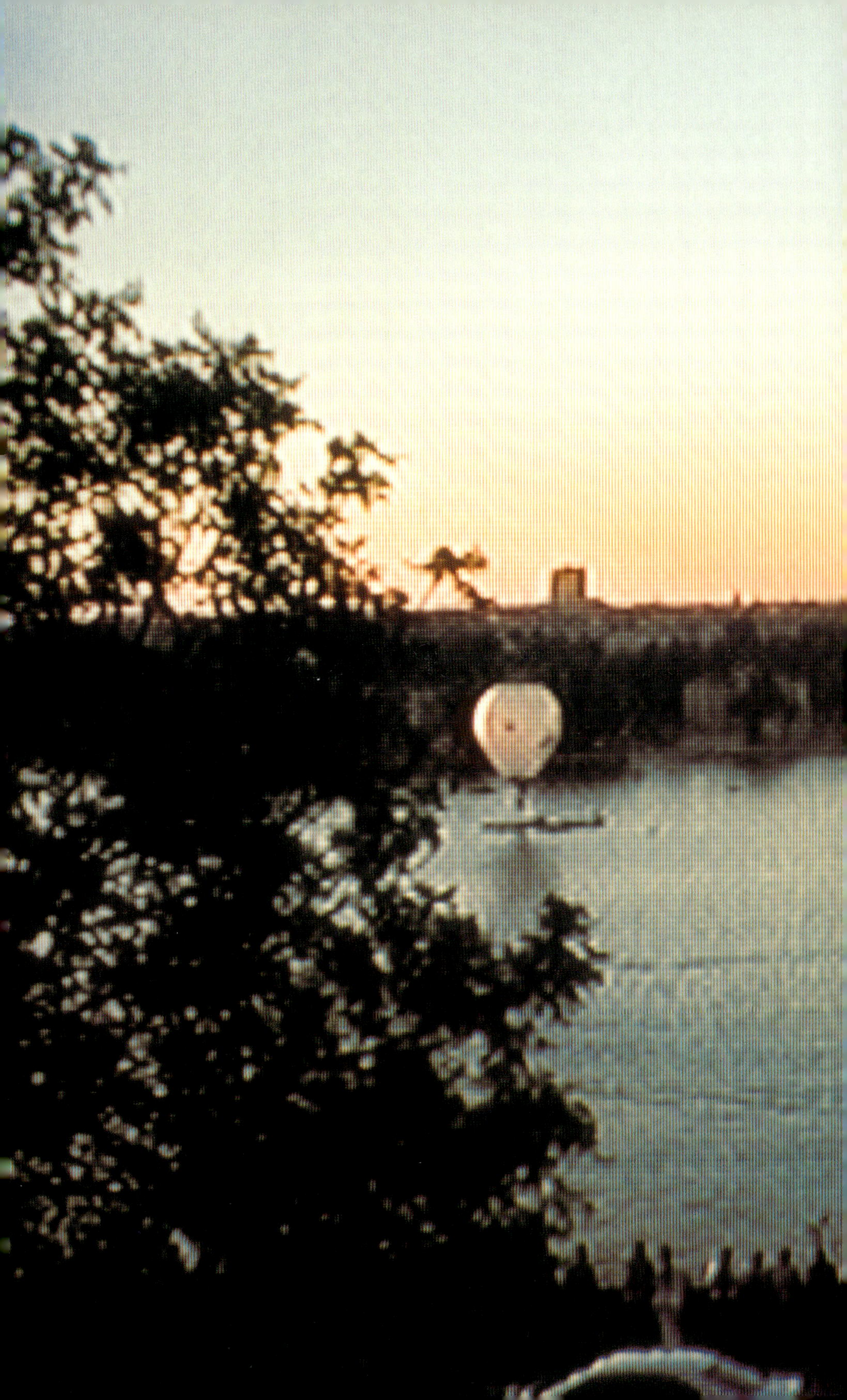

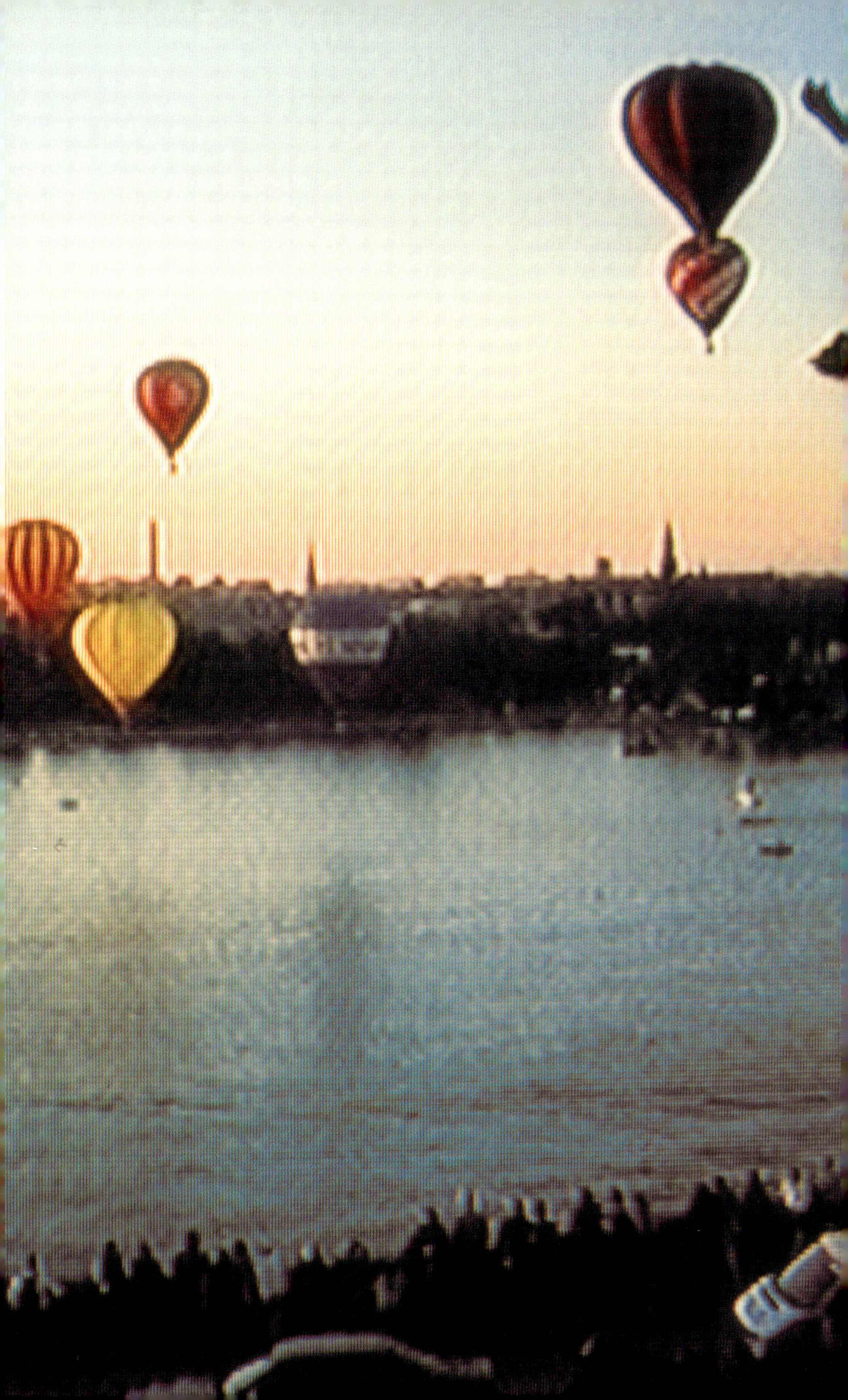

A cosmology for Anne Bjerge Hansen

World
The world is always arriving and departing, forming and dissolving, absent and present. A plunging stone pierces the water's thick green skin. Before our eyes the gaping wound is healed, the incident forgotten. Philosophers ask: if a tree falls unobserved in the isolated depth of a forest, does it make a sound? In order to exist, must the world be witnessed by us? Somewhere, blackberries sway in a light breeze.

Elements and Things
An element is irreducible. It is essential, perhaps eternal. Fire and water. Fire cannot be consumed by fire, nor water drowned by water. Earth and air. They need only themselves. The elements have no core; in their essential, unbounded being they are not things. They may, however, manifest as things under certain circumstances.

> *The stone in the road is a thing, as is the clod in the field. A jug is a thing, as is the well beside the road. But what about the milk in the jug and the water in the well? These too are things if the cloud in the sky and the thistle in the field, the leaf in the autumn breeze and the hawk over the wood, are rightly called by the name of thing.*
>
> Heidegger, *The Origin of the Work of Art*, 1936

It is through things that we understand our relation to the world. The world of things is the world as seen through human consciousness, human reflection. We make things not only for themselves, but also for ourselves. Our relation to things allows us to stand outside the world in a way that is unavailable to animals. From the dog's perspective, a gate is simply an obstruction, an interruption in its passage through space. Birds are alarmed by unspecific noises and by unspecific shapes and movements.

A thing will always remain a thing: its continuing presence introduces time into experience. This thing *is* a thing, *was* a thing and *will continue to be* a thing. Its continuing identity is the partial guarantee of my own identity: I am not it, I will never be it. My existence is separate from its. An aluminium beer barrel bobs and spins desperately in the driving turbulence of a weir. I will it to succeed, to overcome its seemingly hopeless plight. It seems to call for my help. Then I laugh and forget about it.

Tools and Comfort

There is a special class of things called tools, or utensils. A tool or utensil is a thing that will help me achieve an end. It is not simply a thing for itself; it is a thing for me. A glass, jug or cup gives me dominion over the world. It allows me to convert water from element into thing. Once converted into thing, I may consume water (liquidate it) in order to prolong my existence. The effect of the tool makes me think differently about water, it complicates my relation to it. Water is no longer an undifferentiated element, it now enters my consciousness in myriad forms, as a proliferation of things: as the sea, as a river, as rain, as a puddle; as clear and drinkable or stagnant and poisonous; as placid and supportive or violent and destructive. I can understand water as a thing when it is sprinkled from a watering can, poured from a jug or contained in a sink. I am confused when it swills down a playground slide or gushes with unknown interior force from a broken pipe. I am anxious when it spills torrentially over a floodgate.

The tool instigates a double movement. It divides me from the world, establishing the fact that I am here and the world is over there. Simultaneously, however, it allows me to use the world for my own survival, comfort and benefit. Ultimately, it allows me to consume the world. With the plough I can cultivate the earth (turning it into a thing), with the sickle I can harvest the crop, with the oven I can bake bread. With the fence I can define the limits of my proprietorial rights over the world. By turning the tree into timber and the rock into masonry I can build a shelter in which to live. I can build a hearth to domesticate fire, just as I domesticate the horse, the cow, the pig, the chicken, the duck, the cat and the dog. The sweet fruits of the earth, the silent trees, the fragile flowers, the bitter berries, the dancing rivers, the obscure minerals, the stubborn ores, the impassive vegetables: all submit to the law of the tool and the logic of the thing. The world is stripped of magical enchantment and inexplicable astonishment. The shadows are distorted, menacing. They crawl across the wall in slow revolution. There is nothing to be afraid of. Your fears are childish: this is only a little toy house.

Falling and Throwing

Things fall. This may be taken in many ways: things fall, things are fallen, things are thrown. Apples, fragments of glass, confetti, toy pigs, hoops, balls, strips of wallpaper, leaves, flour, avalanches of unrefined chocolate, chips of volcanic rock, a stack of glass tumblers (!) According to Heidegger, we are 'thrown' into the world: it exists before our appearance, it did not invite us. We do not invent our own being, we enter into a Being that is always already present in the world. It is, to some extent, a given, and this given-ness is a problem. It is virtually impossible to conceive of a form of being – of a way of relating to the world – other than the one available. Our acts and thoughts are therefore largely conformist: they fall into line with the acts and thoughts of the majority. We are likely, for example, to think of our self as a thing. Thus we fail to realise our own specific being in the world: we are fallen from the moment we are thrown. The greatest shock, the unwanted reminder: a blur, too fast for the eye to catch. Next: the fallen bird (real or fake?) lies limp in a closed hand.

Time and Place
The world has been purged of its mysteries, its incomprehensible immediacy, its disturbing presence. It has been reduced to a 'thing' to be considered, acted upon, managed, used. It has been subjected to an inflexible regime of time and space, to a relentless logic of cause and effect. The emergence of the thing witnessed the eruption of space – the spaces between self and thing, as well as between one thing and the next. Eventually, such spaces became measurable, accountable, controllable. The fluidity of the world was dissected into a grid of coordinated points. There was to be a place for everything, and everything was to 'be' in its place. Every form was to become fixed, the miracle of metamorphosis at an end. A thing was to be recognised not only by its particular position in space, but also by its particular position in time. A thing was that which occupied this place at this time. Two separate things could not occupy exactly the same place at exactly the same time. The complexities of time itself were subjected to a radical simplification. Time was conceived as a sequence of present moments moving through space, leaving behind a fading trail of pastness. Lost was a sense that time might rise up as much as pass away, that time might be vertical as well as horizontal. That the thing might simultaneously occupy the past, present and future – in a process of coming-to-presence that involved anticipation and recollection – was discounted. The action of the tool on the world – the predictability of its means/ends procedures and cause/effect logic – encouraged the belief that the world itself functioned like a huge machine. Predictability, consistency and logic eclipsed coincidence, arbitrariness and randomness. The swans are content in their disorganised floating and pecking. Why do we smile when they follow the nodding toy duck in tight formation?

Toys and Playthings
Toys are great because they are small. They are things to be played with, rather than things to work with. The toy allows us to play with time and space, freeing them from the logic of means/ends and cause/effect, enabling us to rearrange them at will. In the world of toys, a stack of small wooden rings can be magnified to the scale of architecture. While a toy may take on the dimensions of the real world, the real world may also be incorporated into the world of toys. A helicopter appears in the distant sky, not much more than a speck. Oh no… it's heading straight for the tower! It disappears because of the tower; it disappears because of the toy. It disappears with no consequence, with no ensuing tragedy. Toys: tools to dismantle the false predictability of the world.

Word and Image

Language invaded the spaces between things, equalising those spaces, equalising those things, subjecting them to the imperatives of one-dimensional time. Language is yet another tool enabling us to manage an otherwise unruly world. In the momentum of the sentence, each word is erased by the next. The noun impersonated the thing, became confused with the thing, usurped the thing. Rather than each thing basking in its plenitude, it became condensed to a point of reference for language. If it failed to find a place in language, the thing failed to exist. Language reduced the thing to a sign, no different in character from any other sign. Consequently, the world became a thesaurus of equivalents, of arbitrary correspondences. The task of the word is to ferry meanings, like passengers and cargo, across the deep distances between us and isolated things.

The image shared language's law of equivalence and correspondence, but it remained closer to the thing's complex relation to time. Unlike language, which disintegrates in the wake of time's arrow, the image persists in time. It is simultaneously available to us in its totality. The eye can return to a part of the image it has seen before, making a nonsense of language's irreversibility. Neon signs mock the word's temporality, letting it unravel like luminous twine, only to abruptly rewind it in a cycle of infinite repetition. In language, a pear and a light-bulb retain their difference, their separate locations. In the image, we note their kinship, their overlapping. These correspondences offered by the image reintroduce some of the complexity jettisoned by language. But the image itself is an illusion, a conjuror's trick, a magician's screen, as dazzling, mesmerising and thrilling as a firework in the night. See, here, how it gently spins away, how it slowly sinks beneath the clear surface. It is, never the less, tenacious. Look how easy it is to sweep its tattered strands aside: but see how impassively it gathers itself again. The image of the jockey on the horse eventually reasserts itself, just like the punctured green skin of the inscrutable water.

Epilogue

What do we call that which fills an interval, which restores meaning to the emptiness between things? An Interlude: "a short piece introduced between the acts of the mysteries."

John Calcutt

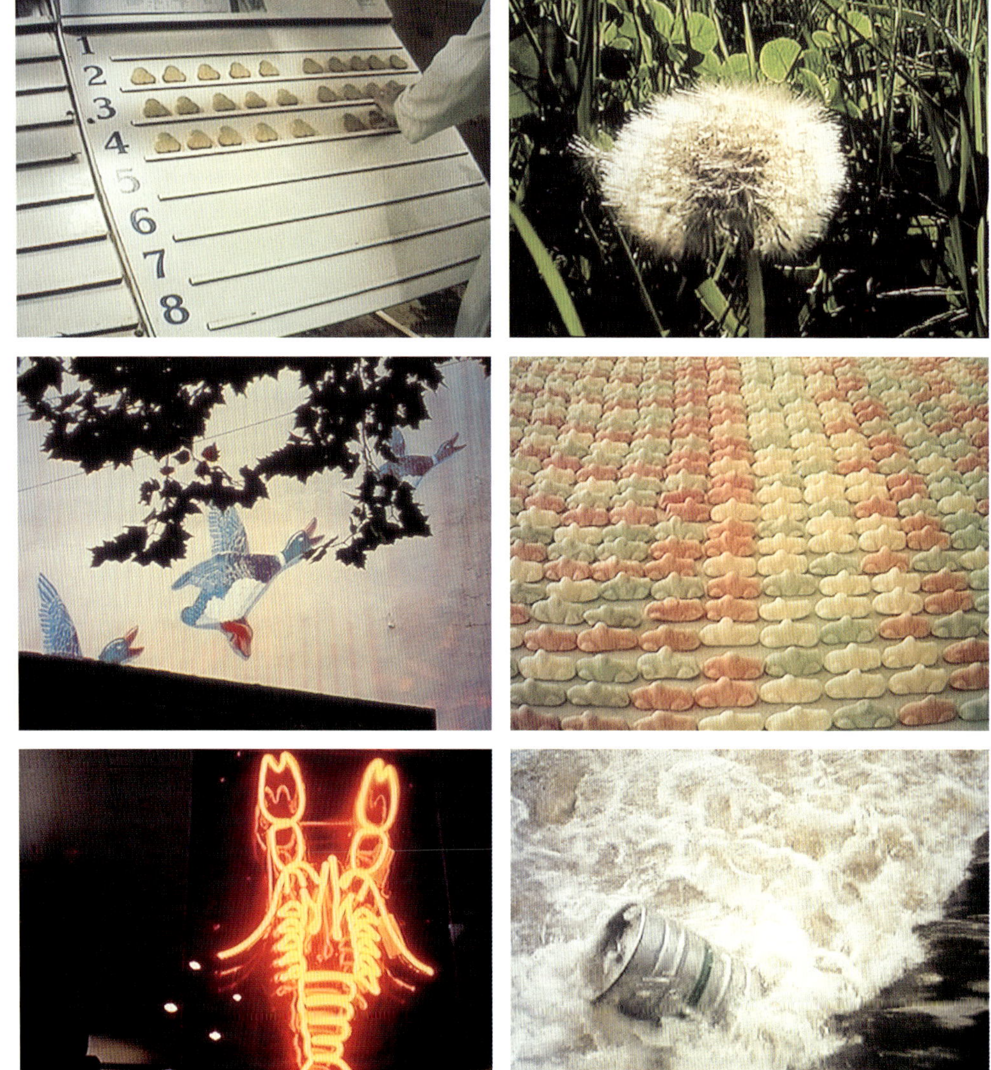
1
2
3
4
5
6
7
8

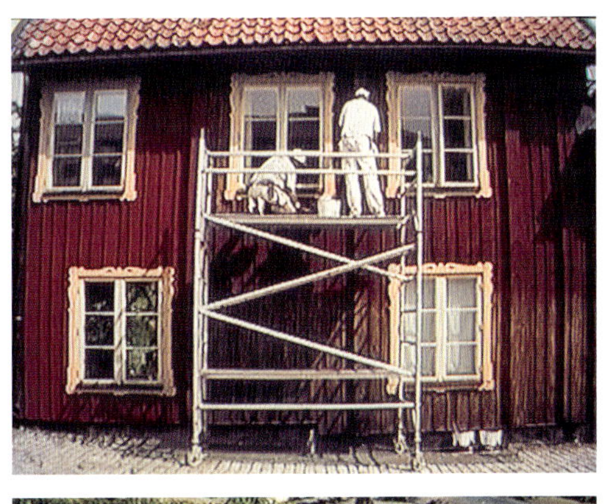
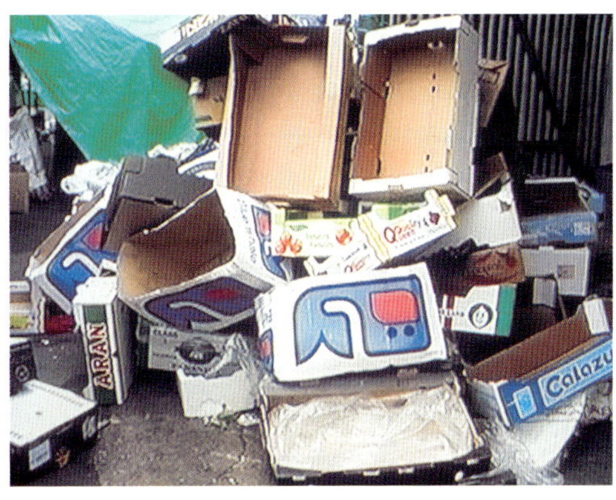
ARAN
Calazu
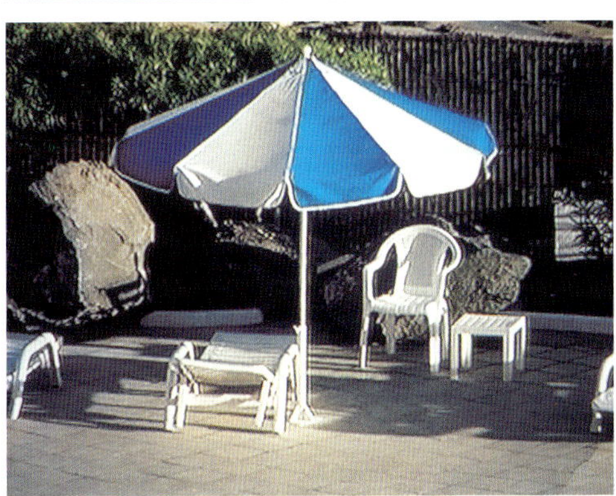
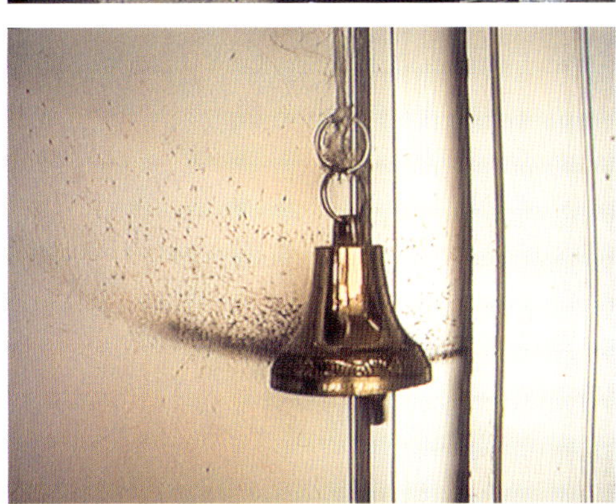
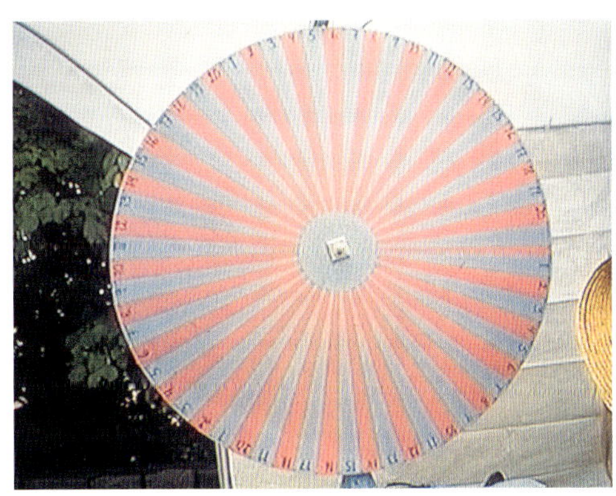
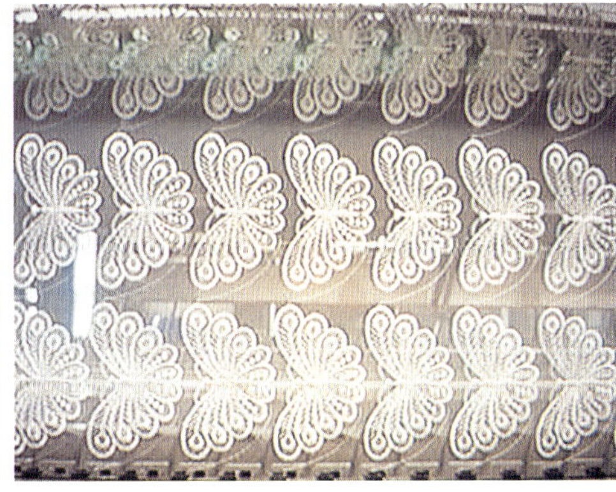

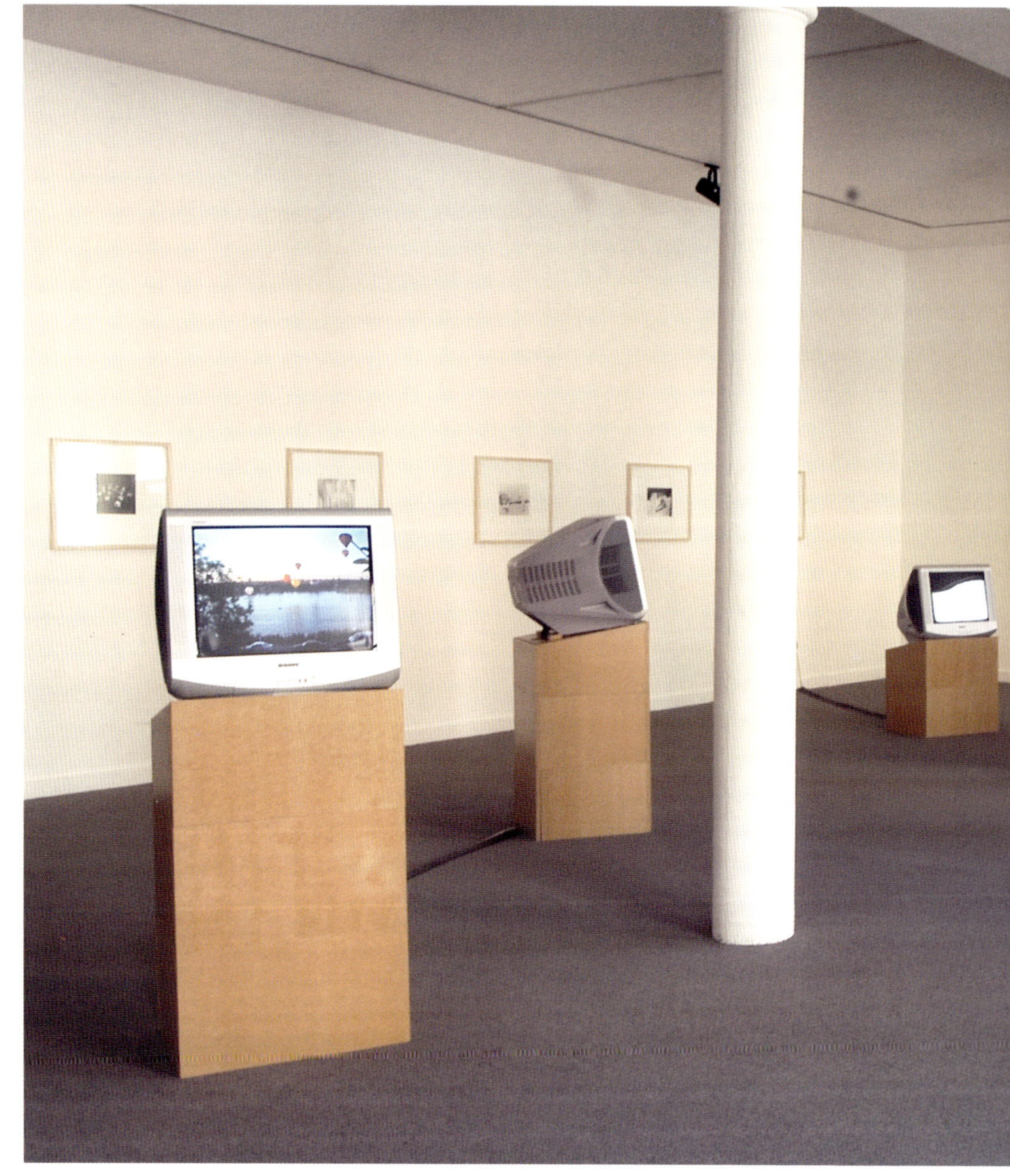

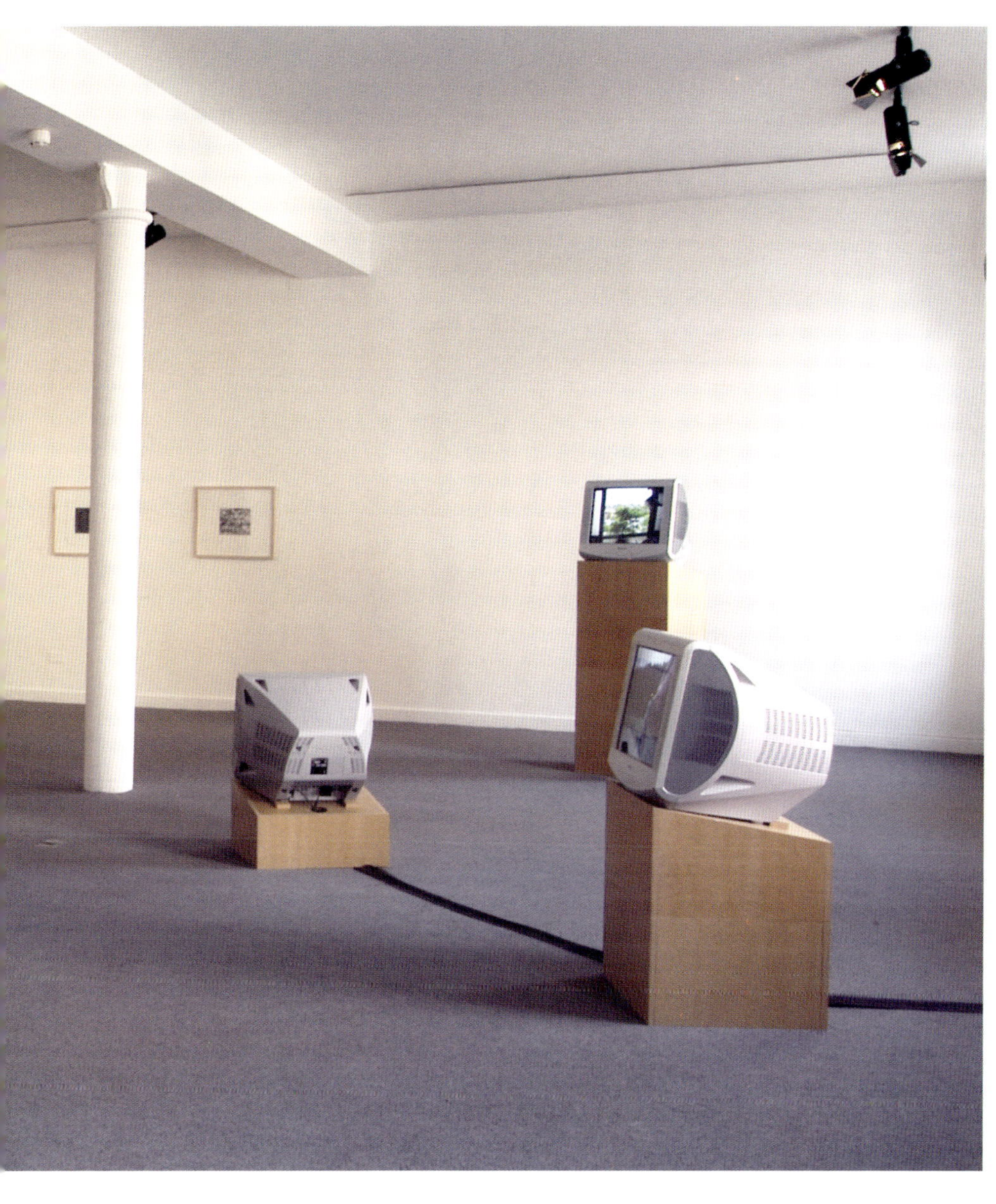